THE GENERATIVE ARTIFICIAL INTELLIGENCE TSUNAMI

Ketaki Karnik, a corporate strategist and policy analyst with two-and-a-half decades of experience, specializes in assessing the impact of evolving zeitgeists on business. Her passion lies in harnessing advanced technology to tackle the wicked challenges facing organizations and nations.

Author of *Secrets for Thriving in the Gig Zone*, a widely recognized guide to success in the gig economy and a Kala Literature Awards finalist, Ketaki also writes fiction. Twice honoured with the South Asia Prize for Micro-fiction and author of three thrillers, she blends sharp analytical insight with a flair for storytelling.

Ketaki holds an MBA from the University of Oxford and loves her guitar, detective fiction and chocolates.

PRAISE FOR THE BOOK

In these times of utter confusion about the impact that AI will have on our society in the coming years, Ketaki Karnik's book provides a valuable template to first understand its potential impact on business and then devise mechanism to address them both at the level of the organization and a manager. The ten megatrends presented in the book are worth watching out for. From the structure of organizations to personal competencies needed for the new world, the book lucidly explains how to prepare for this world of AI and automation. Karnik laces her nuanced arguments with examples from a variety of sectors. Most importantly, she forces us to confront the challenges head-on and provides a means to adapt our ways of thinking and doing in organizations. Must listen to her!

– **Professor Pankaj Chandra**, Vice Chancellor, Ahmedabad University and former Director, Indian Institute of Management Bangalore

The Generative Artificial Intelligence Tsunami is a groundbreaking exploration that uncovers ten transformative trends and delves into the profound impact of generative AI on industries, from automation and personalized customer experiences to intelligent decision-making and AI-driven product development. It provides invaluable insights, practical strategies, and real-world case studies, making it an essential guide for business leaders, entrepreneurs, and policymakers navigating the AI revolution.

What sets this book apart is its India-centric approach, addressing the unique challenges and opportunities within the country's fast-evolving economy. It serves as a strategic blueprint for leveraging AI's potential to drive innovation, efficiency, and competitive advantage. Whether you're a startup founder or a corporate leader, this book offers a clear vision of how generative AI can be a catalyst for success in the digital era. A must-read for anyone looking to stay ahead of the curve!

– **Manish Sabharwal**, Vice Chairman, TeamLease Services Limited

The contours of business have undergone significant change since GenAI tools became available. While corporations are busy coping with its short-term implications, in this thought-provoking book Ketaki Karnik provocatively proposes ten long-term implications of GenAI for the organization. While no one has clairvoyance, this book will enable business leaders to generate energetic debate to make them better prepared for the exciting future ahead.

– **Rishikesha T. Krishnan**, Ram Charan Chair Professor in Innovation and Leadership, Director and Professor of Strategy, Indian Institute of Management Bangalore

THE GENERATIVE ARTIFICIAL INTELLIGENCE TSUNAMI

KETAKI KARNIK

Om Books International

First published in 2025 by

Om Books International

Corporate & Editorial Office
A-12, Sector 64, Noida 201 301
Uttar Pradesh, India
Phone: +91 120 477 4100
Email: editorial@ombooks.com
Website: www.ombooksinternational.com

Sales Office
107, Ansari Road, Darya Ganj,
New Delhi 110 002, India
Phone: +91 11 4000 9000
Email: sales@ombooks.com
Website: www.ombooks.com

Copyright © Ketaki Karnik 2025

ALL RIGHTS RESERVED.

The views and opinions expressed in this book are those of the author, and have been verified to the extent possible, and the publishers are in no way liable for the same. No part of this book may be reproduced or transmitted in any form by any means, electronic or mechanical, including photocopying and recording, or by any information storage and retrieval system, except as may be expressly permitted in writing by the publisher.

ISBN: 978-93-6395-082-5

Printed in India

10 9 8 7 6 5 4 3 2 1

*For dearest Aai and Baba, for training me to unplug
from the conventional dataset, and fuelling my
hunger for the mind-bending*

CONTENTS

	Foreword	xi
1.	Introduction	1
2.	R.I.P., the Organizational Pyramid: Viva, the Hammer-shaped Organizational Structure	21
3.	The Fall and Rise of Small Businesses	44
4.	The World Revolves Around You	74
5.	Unpredictability and Irrationality: The Secret Ingredients of Competitive Strategy	96
6.	The Treasure Hunt for Trivia	112
7.	Experience: The Great Comeback	127
8.	The Clinically Empathetic Organization	138
9.	Trust: The Hallmark of a Winner	148
10.	IQ: For Whom the Bells Toll	165
11.	Bring Your Avatar to Work	182
12.	Conclusion	204
	Acknowledgements	210

FOREWORD

The Generative Artificial Intelligence Tsunami by Ketaki Karnik dives deep into the seismic shifts being brought about by Generative Artificial Intelligence (Gen AI) within the Indian business landscape. The book deftly navigates through ten transformative trends that are set to reshape the foundations of organizations and industries, redefining corporate strategy, competitive dynamics, and work culture.

Gen AI isn't merely an incremental improvement over existing data technologies; it's a revolutionary force capable of generating new data by identifying patterns and characteristics in existing datasets. This transition from traditional data manipulation to Gen AI's capacity for creation marks a pivotal juncture in technology's evolution. The book articulates how these developments will influence business structures, strategies, and the essential skills required to thrive in this new era.

The book stands out for its acute focus on the ramifications of Gen AI within the Indian business context, a topic less frequently explored with such depth and specificity. Unlike other works that primarily discuss Gen AI's technical capabilities, Karnik's book connects these capabilities to actionable insights and trends that will directly impact businesses and professionals. The inclusion of strategies for leveraging these trends provides practical guidance, making it a valuable resource for executives and managers alike.

The Generative Artificial Intelligence Tsunami is especially timely for the Indian context, as organizations across industries - from small ventures to global conglomerates – gear up to integrate Gen AI into their operations. Managers and decision-makers will find the book useful as they design strategies to derive value from the paradigm shift, thereby unlocking exponential gains in competitive advantage.

Another distinctive aspect is its broad applicability. While the primary audience is corporate professionals, the insights are relevant across various types of organizations, including non-profits and academic institutions.

Arguably, the most profound impact of Gen AI is on the corporate professional. The technology could be either a threat to individuals, or an opportunity to leap-frog the career ladder. Replete with pragmatic recommendations, the book lays out a pathway for executives to succeed in the Gen AI era.

Ketaki Karnik, the author, is a seasoned corporate veteran with over two decades of wide-ranging and cross-functional experience. Her extensive career has given her a unique vantage point to assess the transformative potential of advanced technologies like Gen AI. Karnik leverages her wealth of experience and deep understanding of corporate dynamics to offer a compelling narrative and actionable insights that are both forward-looking and grounded in practical reality.

As someone who has witnessed and been part of the technology evolution over the past five decades, I find *The Generative Artificial Intelligence Tsunami* to be a thought-provoking and essential read. It captures the essence of Gen AI's disruptive potential and offers a clear roadmap for businesses to navigate and harness the impending transformations. This book is not just about understanding technology; it's about preparing for a future where adaptability and innovation are paramount.

Bhaskar Pramanik
Former Chairman, Microsoft India
Former Board Member, State Bank of India

CHAPTER 1

INTRODUCTION

There once was a tech quite renowned,
Generative AI, so profound.
It dreamed up new things,
With bytes and with strings,
A creative force unbound!

Love the limerick? Curious about the author? It's ChatGPT, on being prompted to *"create a limerick that defines generative artificial intelligence!"*[1]

In barely a handful of years, Generative Artificial Intelligence (Gen AI) – with ChatGPT as one of its most visible applications – has stormed into our collective consciousness. The disruption has only just begun. It's poised to reinvent the way we think and act. A Salesforce study

---

1   Created and retrieved on 30 March 2024

found that a whopping 73 per cent of surveyed Indians use Gen AI.[2] Interestingly, this figure for India is strikingly higher than in other countries (45 per cent for USA, 29 per cent for the UK). While one can debate the sampling methods, the overall message is clear: Gen AI is here.

It's no exaggeration to say that Gen AI is the black swan event of our time. First referenced by Juvenal, the Roman satirist, in Satire VI,[3] and later popularised by Nassim Nicholas Taleb,[4] a *'black swan'* refers to a rare event with a game-changing impact. Few outcomes could be considered more earth-shattering than the possible extinction of the human race – a scenario espoused by the British-Canadian computer scientist, Geoffrey Everest Hinton. Often called the *'Godfather of Artificial Intelligence,'* Professor Hinton believes there's a 10 per cent chance that AI could cause human extinction within the next three decades.[5] To put that in perspective: if you're 35 years old today, you would be lucky to live past being middle aged!

---

2 'Top Generative AI Statistics for 2024', Salesforce, September 2023. Generative AI Statistics for 2024 - Salesforce

3 Encyclopedia Britannica, Black swan event | Definition, History, Examples, & Facts | Britannica

4 As a result of his book 'The Black Swan : The Impact of the Highly Improbable Paperback', first published 17 April, 2007 by Random House, Allen Lane.

5 'AI could pose 'extinction-level' threat to humans and the US must intervene, State Dept.-commissioned report warns', CNN, 12 March 2024. AI could pose 'extinction-level' threat to humans and US must intervene, report warns | CNN Business

Professor Hinton isn't alone in his concerns. Many other prominent and knowledgeable experts echo a similar view, as reflected in a statement released by the Centre for AI Safety,[6] signed by Sam Altman (CEO, OpenAI, the company behind ChatGPT); Bill Gates; Kevin Scott (CTO, Microsoft); Bruce Schneier (internet security and cryptography pioneer); top executives and researchers from Google DeepMind (Google's AI research laboratory) and Anthropic (leading AI research company), amongst others. Stalwarts like Elon Musk have also raised red flags.

Despite the doomsday scenario, Gen AI is the quintessential double-edged sword. Its utility and revolutionary potential extends across diverse fields: from creative arts to software programming, scientific research to gaming, education to healthcare.

The world of business – the focus of this book – is yet another area where Gen AI promises (or threatens, if you are a tech-antagonist, depending on your perspective!) to overhaul, and unleash a disruptive tsunami. At a micro, operational level, the changes catalysed by Gen AI are well-understood and widely accepted. But the broader, macro-level impact? That's still being debated.

This book identifies ten mega trends primed to reshape the business landscape—their profound implications for the Indian corporate sector as well as corporate professionals.

Let's kick off with a brief primer on the realm of Gen AI.

---

6 'Statement on AI Risk', Centre for AI Safety, Statement on AI Risk | CAIS (safe.ai)

DEMYSTIFYING THE GEN AI UNIVERSE

It's a universally accepted fact that technologists are enamoured by jargon and abbreviations ☺ The world of Artificial Intelligence (AI) is no different.

At its simplest, traditional data technologies work by playing around with existing data – manipulating it at superhuman speeds. These systems rely on algorithms and water-tight instructions provided by a human software programmer. For instance, depending on the sophistication of the computer processor, a system can churn through millions of customer records, and serve up complex data analysis at the click of a button—sales by gender, region, customer age, and any other configuration that catches your fancy, all in under a second.

The catch? The process must be ironclad, with every step of the analysis unambiguously codified in precise logic and rules. 'Garbage in, garbage out'—the old adage captures this perfectly: the system will follow your instructions to the letter, whether they make sense or not.

Pathbreaking technology, indeed! Just think of day-to-day life 30 years ago versus today. Online banking, near-instant searches, video calls on mobile phones, social media, customer analysis, supply chain tracking — the ways our lives have been revolutionized are countless. Yet, despite these advances, the technology is still nowhere close to human intelligence.

Artificial Intelligence seeks to bridge that gap — enabling machines to mirror human intelligence and problem-solving capabilities. The term 'Artificial Intelligence' was first coined in 1956 by John McCarthy, Marvin Minsky, Nathaniel Rochester, and Claude Shannon, in a proposal for a research workshop at Dartmouth College. Although this now-seminal conference is considered the official birth of AI as a field, the idea itself traces back to Alan Turing's 1950 paper *Computing Machinery and Intelligence*[7] which posed the provocative question: *"Can machines think?"*

The broad domain of AI is typically categorised based on two factors: its capabilities and the underlying technologies that drive it.

From a capability perspective, AI is sub-divided into three categories:

1. Artificial Narrow Intelligence (ANI), also known as Weak Artificial Intelligence

As the name suggests, ANI systems are designed for a specific and singular task. They operate within a narrow set of constraints. Clearly, ANI does not match the breadth of human intelligence. What it does is mirror human behaviour (minus the emotions!) in a particular context.

Take for example systems designed to play — and often win — games like chess or the ancient, supremely complex Go. Consider Deep Blue, the computer that famously defeated chess grandmaster and world champion Garry Kasparov in 1997,[8] by evaluating millions of possible future moves to select the most optimal next tactic.

---

7 'Computing Machinery and Intelligence', A. M. Turing, 1950, Computing Machinery and Intelligence (iitd.ac.in)

8 'AI's Victories in Go Inspire Better Human Game Playing', Scientific American, 13 March 2023. AI's Victories in Go Inspire Better Human Game Playing | Scientific American; 'Deep Blue defeats Garry Kasparov in chess match', History, 7 May 2021, Deep Blue defeats Garry Kasparov in chess match (history.com)

As impressive as Deep Blue was, the system could not perform any other task — not even playing a simple game like tic-tac-toe, or distinguishing between a human and a T-Rex.

All current AI systems fall into the ANI category, including those that leverage Machine Learning and Generative AI (both of which are explained later in this chapter). Some common applications of ANI include virtual assistants like Amazon's Alexa or Apple's Siri, and facial recognition software used in surveillance or by social media platforms to tag photos.

2. Artificial General Intelligence (AGI), also known as Strong Artificial Intelligence

AGI systems mirror human intelligence and behaviour. Like you and me, AGI machines would be able to function autonomously—assimilating data from their surroundings and discerning key elements to react appropriately in any situation, including solving challenges—making them almost indistinguishable from humans.

Some sophisticated AI systems might appear to have attained AGI. However, the apparent 'understanding' they display—giving the impression of AGI—is based on learning from the vast data they've been fed (referred to as 'large language models'). In other words, the system's responses depend entirely on the data it receives and are not a product of independent thinking.

Another reason some believe the AGI era has begun is that certain systems have passed the Turing test. Originally dubbed the 'imitation game' by its creator, Alan Turing, the test aimed to measure a computer's ability to 'think.' It involved tasking a human interrogator with distinguishing between a computer and a human within a specified time, based solely on their responses to questions. However, whether these systems truly passed the test is hotly debated. Skeptics argue that the circumstances were limited, and imitating human responses without understanding emotions cannot be considered passing the test. AGI, after all, isn't about replicating responses derived from gigantic amounts of data. It's about cognitive autonomy.

As of now, we are still far from creating an AGI system. Fujitsu, in an attempt to demonstrate AGI, built 'K,' one of the fastest supercomputers in the world. 'K' took forty minutes to mimic one second of neural activity![9] The Chinese-designed Taichi chiplet, powered by light instead of electricity, seems more promising. Scaling this modular chiplet could result in a powerful system capable of being trained as an AGI.

3. Artificial Super Intelligence (ASI)

ASI is the fodder for dystopian science fiction plots. Not only does the AI system develop human-like consciousness, but it also surpasses human intelligence. Think HAL, the AI system aboard the spaceship *Discovery*, in Arthur C. Clarke's *Space Odyssey* series. Upon learning that his human crew intends to disconnect him, HAL proceeds to murder each of his human passengers. (HAL proponents might argue that HAL was merely following a directive that placed the mission above human life, but that's a matter for a separate discussion!)

---

9 'Flash-Forward: What is Artificial General Intelligence?', Business World Innovative Technologies, 2 February 2023, What is Artificial General Intelligence? - A Guide | BWIT (businessworldit.com)

The advent of ASI—if it does emerge—will mark the end of humans as the dominant species on Earth. Fans of Arnold Schwarzenegger's *Terminator* series will recall that Skynet, a synthetic intelligence system (read: ASI), perceived humans as a threat to its existence and, therefore, sought to wipe out humanity. Until then, sleep peacefully…

Moving on from a capability-based classification to a technology perspective of AI. Imagine an AI sophistication spectrum, with Machine Learning at one end and Gen AI at the other. Deep Learning lies between the two.

1. **Machine Learning** (ML) sits at one end of the AI sophistication spectrum. Unlike traditional systems, ML technologies eliminate the need for explicit programming by humans. Instead, these systems create algorithms based on labelled or structured data provided to them, along with highlighted distinctive features. ML systems require vast training datasets to enable learning.

    For example, suppose you need to identify limericks from a collection of poems. ML requires you, the researcher, to supply the system with a training dataset comprising millions of classified poems ('this is a limerick,' 'this is not a limerick'). You also need to highlight the defining characteristics ('five-line stanzas,' 'first, second, and fifth lines rhyme,' etc.). By comparing the classified dataset with the defining features, the ML system creates an algorithm to detect limericks. Once the initial algorithm is applied, the system attempts to classify a new set of data. A human researcher then reviews the output for accuracy and points out errors. The system then modifies its algorithm (this is the learning phase), and the process repeats until the system achieves an acceptable level of accuracy.

ML systems are also used to classify videos. For instance, if you want the system to select dog videos, large numbers of labelled videos are fed to the system along with defining characteristics of dogs (barks, four legs, two ears, etc.). The process is similar to teaching an actor a dance sequence: practice, practice, practice until he gets it right!

In general, ML is used in prediction, classification, and recommender systems. Given historical data, ML can forecast future trends. Specific applications include sales projections, demand forecasts, and weather predictions, among others. ML's classification capability is applied in diverse fields, from fraud detection to spam filtering. Recommender systems supercharge customized marketing to the next level. Analysing your historical choices of movies and series helps your favourite OTT platform suggest other programs personalized to your preferences and tastes.

2. Now, consider a situation where the system is smart enough to identify the defining characteristics by itself, without human intervention. The system independently gleans patterns, which are then used to classify data. This is **Deep Learning** (DL). Continuing with the earlier ML illustrations, the human researcher no longer needs to input characteristics such as 'five-line stanzas,' 'first, second, and fifth lines rhyme,' etc., to identify a limerick, or 'barks,' 'four legs,' 'two ears,' etc., to discern a dog video.

The most prominent and much-talked-about application of DL is autonomous vehicles. DL underpins accident prevention and passenger safety by powering applications such as object detection on the road (e.g., other vehicles, road barriers, lamp posts, road dividers, etc.), lane tracking, and pedestrian tracing.

3. Let's take the limerick example to an epic level. What if AI could not only identify a limerick but also create one? Welcome to **Generative Artificial Intelligence** (Gen AI) – creating based on learning from training datasets. Given access to Shakespeare's works, Gen AI can produce a new piece in Shakespearean style. Even maestros might find it difficult to distinguish between 16th- and early 17th-century Shakespeare and 21st-century Gen AI Shakespeare wannabe. This capability spans multiple media: from text to images, video to software code.

MUCH ADO ABOUT NOTHING?

Fascinating as Gen AI sounds, the real question is whether it's more hype than practical utility. Creating a work in the style of Salvador Dali in 2024 or completing a part-finished movie is cool, but does it add tangible value? The answer, even today—despite the nascent stage of Gen AI on the maturity curve—is a resounding yes. In fact, Gen AI is already causing discontinuous shifts across diverse fields, from the creative to the logical, and everything in between.

Below is a sample of applications spanning different spheres:

1. **Business**: Customisation and productivity enhancement across functions

2. **Culture**: Art and music generation, augmenting or, in some cases, substituting human effort
3. **Education**: Creating personalised learning pathways to ensure higher effectiveness
4. **Gaming**: Making non-playable characters (characters not controlled by players) more adaptive and facilitating greater customisation of avatars and playable characters
5. **Healthcare**: Analysing drug interactions to predict drug-to-drug reactions, thereby ensuring medical professionals make safe drug recommendations based on the patient's medical history and other medications
6. **Meteorology**: Harnessing Gen AI based systems such as Scalable Ensemble Envelope Diffusion Sampler (SEEDS) to generate weather prediction scenarios at scale and at much lower costs than traditional forecasting models
7. **Research & Development**: Expediting and lowering the cost of drug discovery, including proposing potential drugs based on analysing chemical and biological information
8. **Technology**: Automated software code generation, reducing cost and production time cycles
9. **Virtual Assistants**: Introducing natural language processing (ability of computers to comprehend the nuances of human language) capabilities to enhance utility of chatbots

THE POWER OF TOGETHER

Gen AI, by itself, has the potential to revolutionize our lives while raising serious existential questions: if machines have breached the bastion of creation and imagination, sometimes producing outputs that surpass human-made work, then what is our unique value? Philosophical considerations aside (though they certainly deserve a separate discussion), the rise of complementary technologies—predominantly 'deep tech,'[10] as they are commonly known—further amplifies the impact of Gen AI. Combining deep tech with Gen AI is redefining our paradigm: not only promising to expedite and lower the cost of existing activities but, more importantly, offering a range of new applications.

Eight crucial technologies that boost and extend the capability of Gen AI:

1. **Robotics and Internet of Things (IoT), or Internet of Robotic Things (IoRT)**: Merging robotics (machines that automate physical processes) with IoT (internet-connected devices enabling device-to-device or device-to-cloud interaction without human intervention).

2. **Big data**: Storing and analysing data characterised by volume (vast amounts), velocity (speed of data generation, often generated in real time), and variety (different sources and formats such as text, images, etc.).

3. **Cloud Computing**: Undertaking big data analytics requires massive storage space and high-speed

---

10 Abbreviation for 'deep technologies'

processing capabilities. Cloud computing—storing and analysing data on the cloud (the internet)—eliminates the need for expensive and high-end on-site systems, thereby driving economies of scale in big data analytics.

4. **Blockchain**: A decentralised, distributed digital ledger or database that stores records and any modifications to them. The primary advantage is the assurance of transparency in transactions and security (the inability to modify historical records).

5. **Augmented Reality (AR) and Virtual Reality (VR)**: Allowing users to experience interactive, first-hand simulations of scenarios and 3D models.

6. **Quantum computing**: An alternative computational framework using qubits instead of the bits used in classical computing, which enables solving complex problems that classical computers or supercomputers are unable to (or solve them much quicker). Typically, such problems involve large range of variables and creating multiple scenarios.

7. **Natural Language Processing (NLP)**: A subfield of AI that enables computers to comprehend and interpret the nuances of human language.

8. **Vision and speech recognition**: Technologies that enable computers to process, interpret, and understand visual and audio data.

SPOTLIGHT: THE ARENA OF BUSINESS

Business is among the biggest beneficiaries of Gen AI. The transformative potential of the technology spans practically every function within an organization. Early signs of its impact are already evident and widely recognised. It's hardly surprising that Gartner estimates enterprise adoption of Gen AI to grow exponentially — from 5 per cent in 2023 to an overwhelming 80 per cent of companies by 2026[11], at a global level.

In India, businesses are demonstrating strong acceptance of Gen AI, suggesting the country will be among the pioneers in leveraging the technology. A Salesforce study highlights that 91 per cent of companies in India [12] are exploring ways of using Gen AI[13]. Even more encouraging is the response from employees, with 93 per cent of the workforce "excited over the prospect of using Gen AI at work."

This exceptionally rapid growth trajectory is driven by Gen AI's ability to deliver a combination of at least two (often all three) outcomes: enhanced efficiency and productivity

---

11 'Gartner Says More Than 80 per cent of Enterprises Will Have Used Generative AI APIs or Deployed Generative AI-Enabled Applications by 2026', Gartner, 11 October 2023. Gartner Says More Than 80 per cent of Enterprises Will Have Used Generative AI APIs or Deployed Generative AI-Enabled Applications by 2026

12 Of those surveyed by Salesforce

13 '93 per cent of Indian workers excited to use generative AI: Salesforce', The Hindu Business Line, 11 May 2023. 93 per cent of Indian workers excited to use generative AI: Salesforce - The Hindu BusinessLine

(including expediting processes), cost savings, and unlocking new, previously unavailable avenues for value creation and growth. A few illustrations are set out below.

1. Customer experience

- Customised recommendations for potential customers, leading to a higher conversion rate and reduced customer acquisition costs for organizations.
- Combining individual customer preference identification (through Gen AI) with Augmented Reality to introduce virtual fitting rooms for clothes, beauty products, and accessories — boosting purchase propensity and offering a value-add service to both existing and potential customers.

2. Marketing

- Automated and personalised social media content generation, drastically reducing turnaround time (from hours or days to mere seconds) and lowering costs, while enhancing the effectiveness of communication through personalised messaging over generic mass messaging.
- Smart data mining paired with customised messaging, enabling efficient lead generation for new customer acquisition — achieving a higher lead conversion rate and lower customer acquisition cost compared to traditional methods.

3. Operations

- Predictive maintenance that reduces downtime and cuts costs by using models to predict when machines will need servicing and notifying engineers in advance.

- Supply chain optimisation that drives greater efficiency and cost savings.

The power of Gen AI as a lever for strategic, game-changing advantage is undeniable. Organizations that delay or hesitate in adopting it risk being left behind.

WHAT CAN YOU EXPECT FROM THIS BOOK?

Focusing on the business sphere, this book discusses ten pivotal mega-trends, spelling out their implications for the Indian corporate sector and corporate executives.

While much has been written about the operational functionalities of Gen AI, the goal here is to connect the dots between various capabilities to uncover trends that will shape the future of business and individual professionals (managers). How will the overall structure of industries and organizations change? What is the impact on key functions such as customer relationship and marketing? What strategies should organizations adopt to leverage the power of Gen AI? And, importantly, how does it affect you?

Two points of note. First, while these mega-trends are driven by Gen AI, emerging deep technologies help amplify their impact. Second, although the book focuses on the corporate world, these trends are relevant to a wide range of organizations, from non-profits to academic institutions.

Discerned by analyzing the interplay of the corporate context with the power of Gen AI, the mega-trends reshape three fundamental pillars of organizations — industry and organizational structure, corporate and competitive strategy, and people and work culture. Consequently, expect a revolution in how firms navigate their ecosystem, strategize, and operate. Each mega-trend is examined to explore its implications for organizations ("what does it mean for your company?") and professionals ("what does it mean for you?").

A headline view of the ten mega-trends is as under.

Pillar 1: Macro structure of the organization and industry

MEGA TREND #1

R.I.P., the organizational pyramid. Viva, the hammer-shaped organizational structure

Gen AI, combined with automation technologies, will result in a thinning of the organizational structure, at the junior and mid-levels. Consequently, the traditional organizational pyramid will give way to the hammer-shaped organizational structure.

MEGA TREND #2

The fall and rise of small businesses

In the short term, limited resources to leverage Gen AI coupled with the emergence of the new-age conglomerates spells the decline of small enterprises. Over time, however, greater technology accessibility and the proliferation of innovative business models will level the playing field between small and large corporations, paving the way for their resurgence.

Pillar 2: Corporate and competitive strategy

MEGA TREND #3

The world revolves around you

Gen AI marks the end of not just mass marketing, but also mass product and service offerings. Hyper-personalisation has arrived.

MEGA TREND #4

Unpredictability and irrationality: The secret ingredient for competitive strategy

In a world of perfect knowledge and analytics, driven by the widespread adoption of Gen AI, only an irrational move could throw the game of corporate strategy off gear, thereby providing the elusive competitive advantage.

MEGA TREND #5

The treasure hunt for trivia

As data and advanced analytics become ubiquitous, cultural and behavioural nuances about customers – the 'soft' and qualitative information - will be the trump card.

MEGA TREND #6

Experience: The great comeback

In the Gen AI era, qualitative insights into customers and markets, beyond textbook knowledge, together with long-standing relationships and trust are the critical differentiators. This calls for experienced hands. Consequently, older professionals will find greater prominence and relevance in the organizational structure, reversing the current trend of a young top leadership.

Pillar 3: People and work culture

MEGA TREND #7

The clinically empathetic organization

Gen AI-powered tools will enable creation of hyper-targeted messaging, tailored to the recipient, resulting in the 'perfect, most persuasive' communication. Perfect, but devoid of authenticity. As a corollary, the expectation for emotional and cultural intelligence in intra-organizational interaction will rise dramatically.

MEGA TREND #8

Trust: The hallmark of a winner

Customer mistrust towards corporates will heighten against a backdrop of sophisticated deep fakes or hallucinations (generation of incorrect results by AI systems). In this context, trust will emerge as a genuine differentiator.

MEGA TREND #9

IQ: For whom the bells toll

Human expertise in traditional IQ-related skills, such as technical knowledge, analytics and interpretation, is being made redundant by Gen AI. Future-ready competencies centre around creativity, imagination and out-of-the-box thinking, amongst others.

MEGA TREND #10

Bring your avatar to work

In the not-too-distant future, your avatar, creating by fusing deep technologies and Gen AI, will attend meetings on your behalf. This clone-like avatar will not only mirror your physical self with near-perfection but also mimic your responses and reactions during discussions.

In what follows, each mega-trend and its consequences are elaborated upon.

CHAPTER 2

R.I.P., THE ORGANIZATIONAL PYRAMID
VIVA, THE HAMMER-SHAPED ORGANIZATIONAL STRUCTURE

> *Generative AI, a marvel to see,*
> *Brought an end to the hierarchy decree.*
> *No more pyramid's climb,*
> *As minds intertwine,*
> *In a network where creativity's free.*
>
> – ChatGPT, on being prompted to "create a limerick on generative artificial intelligence and the end of the hierarchical pyramid organization structure!"[1]

---

1 Created and retrieved on 28 April 2024

> *Gen AI, combined with automation technologies, will usurp many (nearly all, in some cases!) of the activities currently undertaken by humans. Consequently, the lower and middle tiers of the traditional organizational structure will thin out. As a result, the age-old organizational pyramid structure – with more employees at the junior level vis-à-vis its subsequent senior layer – will give way to the hammer-shaped organizational structure.*

THE RATIONALE
A TALE AS OLD AS TIME: THE PYRAMID SHAPED ORGANIZATION

Pyramids, among the most iconic structures of our ancient world, are popularly associated with Egypt. Lesser-known Sudan, however, boasts the largest aggregation of pyramids in the world. In the same vein, while Egypt is home to the most famous pyramids — Giza, along the west bank of the Nile — these monuments are not unique to the two Northeast African nations. Pyramids are found across the globe, from the Nubian pyramids of Sudan to the Mesoamerican pyramids of Mexico; from the Mayan pyramids of Guatemala to the Chinese pyramids of the Qin and Han dynasties. The shape itself finds resonance in structures such as the 10th-century seven-tiered pyramidal temple Koh Ker in northern Cambodia, to the more recent Louvre Pyramid, built in 1989.

Tempting as it may be to attribute the conventional organizational configuration — a broad base of employees at the lower or junior level, gradually reducing as one ascends the hierarchy, forming a triangle or its three-dimensional form, the pyramid — to its physical structure, the timelines, in fact, tell a different story. Tracing the origins of the pyramid-shaped hierarchy is impossible (even for Gen AI!). "As old as time" sums it up perfectly. Since the era of the Sumerians, the earliest known civilization (4100–1750 BCE), to ancient Egyptians (3100–30 BCE), and closer to home, the Indus Valley civilization (3300–1300 BCE), the pyramidal structure of organizations has existed. This ubiquitous structure appears across governance (think: emperor or pharaoh, governors, administrators), military (think: generals, lieutenants, foot soldiers), and social systems (think: ruling royalty, government officials,[2] nobles, and priests), among others.

Modern management philosophies espouse a similar concept. Frederick Winslow Taylor, considered the father of scientific management, in his legendary paper *'The Principles of Scientific Management* (1911)'[3], emphasized the need for clear management hierarchy. Henri Fayol, in his book *'Administration Industrielle et Générale'* (1916),[4] introduced the

---

2   In the Egyptian social structure, government officials were people related to the pharaoh (thus, nobles) and chosen by him / her to serve as an official. Hence, they superseded other nobles and priests.

3   'The principles of scientific management', Frederick Winslow Taylor, first published by Harper & Brothers in 1911, recently published by Dover Publications in 1997

4   'Administration industrielle et générale', Henri Fayol, first published by H. Dunod et E. Pinat in 1917 in French. English translation by Constance Storrs, first published by Sir Isaac Pitman & Sons Ltd in 1949, 2015.13518.General-And-Industrial-Management.pdf (archive.org)

concept of the scalar chain — formal lines of communication and supervision running from the highest to the lowest ranks in an organization — as part of his 14 principles of management.

The rationale behind the pyramid-shaped organizational structure is self-evident: fewer people are needed as you move up the hierarchy. Simplistically, 200 workers are supervised by 15 foremen, who report to 4 shop floor managers, all overseen by a factory or plant head. Visualizing this yields a pyramid.

While the number of layers in the hierarchy (for example, four layers in the illustration above) may vary across organizations, the overall shape remains the classic pyramid. "Flat structures" are currently in vogue, especially among start-ups and new-age firms. But probe deeper, and you'll find the number of levels is reduced, yet the architecture still resembles a pyramid — albeit a flatter version. On the fringes of modern organizational design lies holacracy: fluid, autonomous, self-organizing teams with a clear short-term focus. The concept is still evolving, yet at the firm level, the pyramid persists.

Companies adopt various criteria such as functional (marketing, finance, etc.), geographical (North India, East India, etc.), or brand-centric (economy brands, premium brands, luxury brands, etc.) to organize personnel and operations. Irrespective of the framework implemented, the outcome is consistent: employee strength at the CEO minus two level is higher than at the CEO minus one, a pattern repeated across all layers of the organization. Whether a small firm or a global giant, a manufacturing or services enterprise, the tiered structure remains resolute, forming the backbone of organizational design. Viva the organizational pyramid.

The pyramid framework has stood steadfast through the annals of time, enduring disruptions and game-changing events. Consider revolutionary episodes such as the advent of computerization in the business world or automation on the shop floor. Although the lower layers of hierarchy were trimmed, the overall shape remained intact.

The introduction of computers in the Indian banking system in the 1980s—an inflection point in corporate history—is a specific case in point. Bank unions protested, fearing job losses. Instead, they discovered significant productivity gains and greater ease of working. Tedious tasks such as writing, manually checking, and verifying ledgers were reduced to a fraction of the time, freeing up bandwidth for strategic matters. Functionalities and value-added services could be offered to customers that were previously impossible. Notably, computerization, combined with communication networks, heralded the era of anywhere, anytime banking. Despite the magnitude of the impact, the pyramid shape of the organization endured.

Past transformative events, at most, resulted in the disappearance of a layer of the organizational hierarchy (the typist pool, for instance), but the overall shape remained unchanged. Gen AI, in conjunction with automation, is now poised to shatter this age-old paradigm.

THE UNSTOPPABLE WAVE: AUTOMATION

Automation has reached the tipping point of no return. The derived value is too great to be ignored.

The 'what' of automation

Industry 4.0, a broad term encompassing a combination of deep technologies mentioned in Chapter 1—such as the Internet of Robotic Things (robotics merged the Internet of Things), big data, advanced data analytics, and AI—is often used interchangeably with automation in casual conversation. For the purpose of this discussion, however, 'automation' is the preferred term.

Automation encompasses hardware and software technologies that replace tasks previously performed by humans. Robotic arms welding, assembling, and painting cars exemplify physical automation. Similarly, assembly lines that compresses powder into tablets, followed by packaging and labeling, illustrate automation in the pharmaceutical industry.

The impact on services is equally profound. Customer inquiries are a prime example. Virtual assistants handle routine queries, allowing human customer service teams to focus on more complex issues. A key advantage of automation is its 24x7 availability—even during Diwali and New Year! Finance and accounts, too, have been overhauled, from automated processing to transaction tallying and financial statement generation.

The 'why' of automation

Gains from automation are well understood and broadly fall into four buckets: enhanced productivity through reduction in the time taken to complete processes; higher and consistent quality due to better accuracy and a lower (often nil) error rate; workplace safety; and the potential to offer value-added services or new functionalities to customers. Cost savings, although a prominent benefit, has not been singled out as it often stems from one or a combination of the other four elements. Nevertheless, in certain instances, it can manifest as an independent outcome.

Machines, unlike humans, do not require breaks or changeover time between shifts and, importantly, can operate 24x7, thereby delivering unprecedented levels of performance. Additionally, a reduced labour force yields two ancillary productivity gains: fewer labour issues and reduced compliances.

Labour union disputes and strikes have long been the bane of corporate India (this comment in no way suggests that labour union demands are unreasonable) since 1918, when the country's first workers' union, the Madras Labour Union,[5] was set up. Such disputes have often turned disruptive, with well-intentioned labour laws (necessary to safeguard the rights of the economically weak and marginalized sections of society) being perceived by management as too stringent and one-sided. Unsurprisingly, many company leaders eagerly embrace automation. As machines steadily take over jobs, starting with the lower tiers of the hierarchy, worker headcounts plunge. Fewer workers imply fewer labour disputes, fewer strikes, and improved productivity.

Multiple worker-related regulations also imply a host of compliances and accompanying paperwork (mostly electronic

---

[5] 'Madras Labour Union's fiercest battle', The Hindu, 23 August 2024, Madras Labour Union's fiercest battle - The Hindu

these days). Again, a tedious activity that diminishes with the reduction in the worker force.

On the quality front, automation reduces, if not eliminates, errors, often dropping the rejection rate to zero. Unlike humans, fatigue does not creep in and consistency of delivery is maintained. A study estimates that human errors cause 23 per cent of all downtime.[6]

Human safety is of particular concern in dangerous environments such as underground mines, where the terrain is rough, unpredictable, and traditional communication systems often fail. Tragically, nine fatal mining accidents were reported in India in 2020, each claiming an average of 30 lives[7] - amounting to around 270 lives lost due to hazardous workplaces in the technologically advanced 21st century. Serious, although non-fatal, accidents were in addition.

Automation also enables the introduction of new value-added services or functionalities that were previously unfeasible, boosting both topline and profitability.

Various studies have sought to capture the quantitative impact of automation. One study estimates that organizations will achieve an average cost reduction of 31 per cent by 2025.[8] As an illustration, the study highlights a financial services firm

---

6 'Fully Automated Factories: The Future Of Manufacturing?', OEE systems. Fully Automated Factories: The Future Of Manufacturing? | OEEsystems

7 'How IoT can reduce mining accidents', The Hindu Business Line, 9 July, 2023. https://www.thehindubusinessline.com/business-tech/how-iot-can-reduce-mining-accidents/article67058658.ece

8 'Automation with intelligence', Deloitte Insights, 30 June 2022, Robotic process automation (RPA) | Deloitte Insights

that achieved a 70 per cent cost reduction in its target areas. The extractive industry, too, has benefited, with companies like Boliden (a Swedish mining and metals company) expecting a 40 per cent increase in productivity by automating drill rigs.[9]

Automation: here and now

Against this backdrop, it is unsurprising that the automation bandwagon is already here, with intense efforts underway to accelerate adoption. A whopping 70 per cent of the organizations are at least piloting automation in one or more areas, according to a 2022 survey[10]; this figure would certainly have increased over the past two years. The high trial and adoption rate is further reflected in the fact that many surveyed companies anticipate directing around 25 per cent of their capital spend, until 2027, toward automated systems.[11]

The automation wave is upon us, and the lure is too strong.

THE GRAND DISPLACEMENT

Job displacement is the dark side of automation.

Roles traditionally undertaken by humans are being absorbed by machines or software. A car manufacturing

---

9 'A case study on automation in mining', Ericsson Consumer & IndustryLab, A case study on automation in mining - 5G business value (ericsson.com)

10 'Your questions about automation, answered', McKinsey & Company, 8 July 2022, Automation technologies: Your questions answered | McKinsey

11 'Unlocking the industrial potential of robotics and automation', McKinsey & Company, 6 January 2023, Unlocking the industrial potential of robotics and automation | McKinsey

factory that once teemed with hundreds of welders and painters now hosts a tenth — and soon, even fewer — of the number of humans. Pioneering companies are racing toward fully automated plants, colourfully termed 'lights-out manufacturing.' A Philips plant in the Netherlands, which manufactures electric razors, operates with a mere nine workers.[12] The 3,000-acre campus of Chinese electric vehicle manufacturer Xpeng Motors houses a fully automated plant comprising 264 industrial robots.[13] Low-level call centres have largely been replaced by intelligent software that can perform the same tasks with greater accuracy and higher productivity.

The impact on jobs is staggering. One report estimates 800 million job losses by 2030.[14] A third of the workforce will be impacted in developed economies such as Germany and the United States. Another study forecasts that 60–70 per cent of mine-site roles will become redundant.[15] Estimates for specific companies and roles are even higher. For instance,

---

12 'Fully Automated Factories: The Future Of Manufacturing?', OEE systems, Fully Automated Factories: The Future Of Manufacturing? | OEEsystems

13 'Is this the most highly automated factory in the world?', Robotics & Automation, 23 July 2020, Is this the most highly automated factory in the world? | Robotics and Automation (roboticsandautomationmagazine.co.uk)

14 'Robot automation will 'take 800 million jobs by 2030' - report', BBC, 30 November 2017, Robot automation will 'take 800 million jobs by 2030' - report (bbc.com)

15 'Trend 8: The intersection of talent and community', Deloitte Insights, 3 February 2020, Automation and remote mining's impact on communities | Deloitte Insights

autonomous haulage systems deployed in mines could reduce the need for human drivers by almost 90 per cent.

That said, it is important to highlight that at an overall or macro level, jobs are not being eliminated, merely displaced — and, in some cases, even multiplying. For example, a role scrapped in a call centre providing flight or train timing information generates at least one, or likely more roles, in a technology firm (to develop, maintain, and occasionally upgrade the system) and in an information services company (to ensure accurate real-time information is continuously fed to the automated software system). At the organizational level, however, one role has been chipped off from a relatively junior layer of that structure.

SHAPE SHIFTING
The metamorphosis

Massive job displacements spurred by automation are snipping off layers of the hierarchical pyramid at the firm level. At the very least, they are thinning the pyramid.

Now, add AI — particularly Gen AI — to the mix. Consider the simple, though tedious, task of invoice tallying. Previously undertaken manually, this activity was prone to human error — either inadvertent, due to fatigue (imagine staring for hours at reams of paper filled with figures), or worse, deliberate fraud.

- Step 1: Automation: Even a basic accounting system can extract data from invoices for validation and analytics.

- Step 2: Introduce AI: With AI's pattern detection capabilities, errors — whether accidental or fraudulent — can be identified. Some of this could also be achieved through data analytics or rudimentary AI.
- Step 3: Introduce Gen AI: Building on the output from Step 2, Gen AI translates the findings into natural human language, comprehensible to all. It collates and cogently summarizes the relevant details and arguments to support a recommended course of action. A sample report might read:

"Two instances of fraud detected, each of amount [INR xx]. The invoices were payable to [Fraudster 1] and were generated by employee [Scamster 1] on [date]. The reasons these cases have been identified as frauds, and not human errors, are [reasons]. Given the nature of the fraud, precedents, and the people concerned, the recommended course of action is [xyz]. The actions have been proactively initiated and the status is [xyz]. The system has also checked for other violations by the said employee and found [xyz]."

Layering automation with Gen AI eliminates the need for data operators — typically the junior tier in the finance department hierarchy — and extends all the way up the value chain to analytics experts and junior strategy personnel, who convert data into actions (often part of the mid-level hierarchy). This is just one illustration. Now imagine this model being replicated across other processes and functions within the firm.

The outcome: The number of junior-level employees in an organization reduces drastically, as the broad base of the pyramid collapses into a narrow rectangle — driven more by automation than by Gen AI. With AI, including Gen AI, the middle tier — traditionally responsible for data analytics and interpretation — faces a similar fate.

In effect, organizations will witness a thinning of employees at both the junior and middle layers. Over the next 5–8 years, the senior layer, in terms of the number of people (though not necessarily skillsets or roles), will likely remain largely unchanged. Picture the structure from bottom to top: thin (junior), thin (middle), and a slight bulge (senior or top leadership) — the shape of a **hammer**. To clarify: the slight bulge at the top is not due to an increase in headcount but rather the retention of the status quo. That said, in some cases, there may be a slight increase in personnel at the senior or top leadership level, to bring in specialized expertise.

Who will bell the cat: Pace of change

The transformation from the pyramid to the hammer shape will occur faster than typical organizational paradigm shifts, driven by rapid adoption of automation and AI. In fact, this wave has already been unleashed. The pace of change depends on the nature of the company, specifically the sector it operates in, its customer profile, and its size.

Numerous research studies and thought leadership publications predict which sectors are likely to be early adopters of automation. While automotive, electronics, and pharmaceuticals are emerging as the front-runners, eventually, the automation-AI duo will impact all sectors. Functions, too, will mirror this trend. Conventional wisdom held that creative processes and domains would remain immune to technological advancements. However, Gen AI, with its inventive prowess, has shattered that belief.

Return on investment, both current and anticipated, defines the speed of transformation. Costs must be outweighed by the value derived, whether in the form of higher productivity, better quality or accuracy, additional functionalities, or other positive outcomes. As a general rule, companies specialized in delivering high-end precision or accuracy-based products and services are prime candidates. Export-oriented firms, particularly those serving demanding customers in Europe and the USA, or companies integrated into global value chains, are also major contenders. Their need to deliver superior quality and the customer willingness to pay a reasonable premium drive this transformation.

Low labor costs in India, and across developing economies, raise the threshold for minimum returns. Given the correlation between labor costs and the adoption of deep technologies, the extraction sector in India is expected to lag behind manufacturing and services. The prevalence of illegal mines in commodities like sand, coal, and granite points to vast employment at very low costs, as these entities evade formal employment regulations and costs. For instance, government-mandated minimum wages are inevitably ignored. Automation is more expensive than the cost of informal workers. Furthermore, illegal mines operate in a cash economy, where transactions are predominantly made in cash, contributing to the reluctance to adopt automation.

However, as the furore for miner safety and stricter labor laws takes center stage, the pace of transformation will accelerate.

Broadly speaking, large multinational companies are likely to be the early movers, given their customer profiles and the availability of substantial funds to invest in new technologies. A few mid-sized enterprises will also ride the first wave, particularly those that are part of global value chains or derive a significant portion of their sales from exports. The pace of adoption by company size is further discussed in the trend 'The fall and rise of small businesses.'

A novel aspect of the automation-and-AI combination is its sheer ubiquity, remodelling every function of the organization. While attention often centres on production, where the bulk of the workforce resides, this duo is overhauling even smaller functions like HR. Automation (e.g., "Your self-assessment is due on [date]") paired with AI-based recommender systems (e.g., scanning resumes and publicly available information to create a prioritized shortlist of potential candidates) will amplify productivity while shrinking team size.

We can expect hammer-shaped organizations to take shape over the next 3 to 5 years. By 2028–2030, the majority of larger and more progressive mid-sized organizations will adopt this structure.

JUMP-STARTING YOUR COMPANY

Internal restructuring is more complex than commonly assumed and has the potential to turn into a public relations nightmare. The transition phase, in particular, is the most challenging, akin to designing an aircraft while flying. Change is on the horizon but not yet fully realized.

During this period, it's evident that certain roles will either shift from humans to machines or become redundant within a few years—possibly as soon as two to three years. In the interim, however, these activities still need to be carried out by humans and, therefore, require staffing. The added complication in the case of automation and AI is the rapid pace of change. Historically, tectonic shifts of this nature have taken place over an extended period, providing a long enough runway for gradual adjustments. Gen AI defies this notion.

Outlined below are seven pointers to help your company transition smoothly.

1. Create a transition plan

As obvious as this may seem, the number of companies that fail to develop a detailed plan is surprising.

While there is an overall window for transition, exact timeframes are unclear. In the world of fast-evolving deep technologies coupled with the imperative to deliver tangible returns to demanding stakeholders, one year too late could spell disaster. Scenario creation and the agility to pivot between scenarios is critical. Nevertheless, prepare a blueprint, keeping in mind that it will need to be updated at regular intervals.

2. Form a high-level task-force

The task force for developing and executing the transition plan must include top leadership from across functions. Strategic and tough decisions will need to be made. Diversity in perspective, a rigorous holistic view, and buy-in from all senior management will facilitate smooth implementation.

An external expert, akin to an adjudicator-cum-futurist, could also be co-opted into the task force. With divergent opinions inevitable, an independent, knowledgeable voice will be invaluable. The imminent era is unfamiliar to everyone, and in-house specialists (e.g., the head of HR or production) may not be the best equipped to forecast and plan the transition even for their respective fields.

3. Prepare stakeholders

The importance of preparing and informing stakeholders cannot be overstated. Each key stakeholder may be at a different level of understanding and appreciation of the consequences of Gen AI. Develop and execute a comprehensive communications program that covers all key stakeholders and their specific contexts.

For instance, some board members may not fully grasp the changes that Gen AI heralds; 'education sessions' for such members should be organized. Similarly, investment analysts who use employee strength as one of the parameters to assess company growth (e.g., in the case of BPO firms) might perceive a decline in firm value as the headcount diminishes due to automation and Gen AI. Correct such misconceptions promptly to avoid the risk of your company being downgraded on the stock market or by private equity investors.

Vendors and customers are other major target groups. In the traditional worldview, a reduction in personnel signals deteriorating or declining health for the organization, leading suppliers and clients to panic ("Are we dealing with a failing organization?" "Should we scout for a substitute partner?"). Depending on their level of technological savviness, explaining the new paradigm could be a lengthy, though essential, process. Start immediately and proactively.

4. Smart recruitment

The detailed transition plan highlights vulnerable roles—those that will either be made redundant or usurped by machines. Until the end-state materializes, these activities still need to be carried out by humans. Explore non-permanent modes of filling these positions, such as contractual or gig work. Review the entry-level or campus recruitment requirements.

At the same time, a few positions in certain roles will persist, although the number of openings may drastically decrease—e.g., from 100 help desk executives to 5. Select these five executives smartly and quickly, and, in the words of Don Corleone, 'make them an offer they cannot refuse,' because, like your company, other firms will also compete for the best talent in the market.

The decision becomes tricky for upper-mid level roles that are likely to be axed, yet the timeframes may allow for upward movement into senior leadership. In such cases, the choice between temporary and permanent employees depends on the potential for upward mobility within the hierarchy.

5. Go the extra mile for existing employees

Nothing harms companies more than bad publicity caused by unfairly treated former employees. Be forthright with employees, particularly those likely to be affected, and share updates as clarity emerges regarding high-probability scenarios. Contrary to popular belief among top management, employees are often well-informed about shifts in the business environment. Staying silent can lead to gossip, and may create the impression that inaction on the part of management reflects ignorance.

Undertake a fresh employee calibration exercise from the imminent Gen AI perspective to assess skill fitment and identify potential high performers among existing employees. Keep in mind that the skill sets required in the Gen AI era are drastically different from those valued today (elaborated in a subsequent trend). Therefore, achievers in the current era may not remain the stars of tomorrow—and vice versa.

Retrain vulnerable employees for other roles within your company. Recognize that, depending on your company's growth plans and the skillsets of impacted employees, it may not be possible to absorb all retrenched personnel. Therefore, establish mechanisms to help employees find opportunities outside the organization, such as access to a wide variety of courses, career counseling, and outplacement services.

At the same time, don't forget to reinforce the employees you intend to retain. While organizations may slim down, the battle for talent will intensify.

6. Review operations

Depending on the specifics of your company's operations, the retrenched employee pool could be spread across corporate offices, branch offices, plants, or delivery centers.

Review existing corporate and branch office space to assess real estate needs for the next 3 to 5 years. In plants, increased automation and Gen AI could lead to factory realignments, potentially altering square footage requirements. Additionally, fully autonomous plants could be relocated to less expensive locations, as the need for proximity to workers becomes less relevant.

7. Migrate senior leadership

An obvious consequence of the new era is a reduced span of control (of humans!).

A factory head, who previously had ten managers reporting directly and another 800 reporting indirectly to her, may now have, for example, just two direct reports, with the number of indirect reports shrinking from 800 to 30 (a figure that will decrease further over time). Human egos are fragile and need to be managed! Emphasize that span of control should be measured by tangible product or service output, not by the number of humans reportees.

Board members adhering to the conventional mindset should also be sensitized. Replace their pride in leading a large organization (e.g., a 5,000-person company) with satisfaction of spearheading a significantly smaller, albeit pioneering, firm.

JUMP-STARTING YOUR CAREER

Don't panic – the golden rule!

Your current position in the organizational hierarchy determines the optimal course of action for you.

1. YOU ARE IN THE JUNIOR OR MID TIER OF THE ORGANIZATION

(To clarify, junior or mid tier within your organization, not against an absolute scale)

First, undertake a **realistic assessment** of your role. Will it succumb to automation and Gen AI?

- Assume a 3–5 year horizon. Five years might seem like a long period; however, given the exponential pace of technology adoption, as it reaches its tipping point, the

five-year span could easily shrink to three years. As the saying goes, "objects in the rearview mirror are closer than they appear," so be prepared.
- Do not rely on factors like management lethargy to assume your firm will not transition. Once the momentum builds, all companies will get swept up by the wave. Waiting at the platform for the Mumbai local is a fitting analogy. At peak traffic times, even if you have no experience jostling your way into a train, standing at the right spot on the platform gets the job done.
- Hit the reskill button, even if you estimate low odds for your role being Gen AI-ed. Change is accelerating faster than you think. Choose your focus skills wisely. Expertise and competencies valued today are radically different from those that will dominate the Gen AI era (elaborated in a subsequent trend).

Stay open to newer forms of working, such as gig or contractual. The brave new world values flexibility in its workforce. Companies are uncertain about how the technology game will play out and are cautious about adding permanent staff.

Plan financially and emotionally for re-learning or downtime. Ideally, you would reskill while retaining your current role, then seamlessly transition to a new Gen AI-compatible role. Prepare for the worst—a gap between your current and new job. Along with financial planning, gear up emotionally (you and your loved ones) for a possible employment lag.

One way to gain a slightly longer runway to transition is to **shift to a laggard firm or sector**. The former is a risky route, as stragglers in the automation and Gen AI world may lose the survival battle.

Stay positive: all is not lost. It's possible that a version of your role has simply been displaced to another entity or sector. For instance, you might need to transition from providing engineering inputs in a manufacturing plant to becoming an engineering domain specialist in a technology development company—an opportunity tailor-made for you. The trick is being **open to pivoting roles**.

2. YOU ARE IN THE SENIOR OR TOP MANAGEMENT OF THE ORGANIZATION

You get a breather, but only just!

Re-alignment in the junior and middle layers of the organization could drive a re-jig at the senior level. Roles and responsibilities will be redefined. **Stay flexible**.

Change will trickle up—sometimes faster than you expect—necessitating two actions. First, boost your understanding of the implications of AI and Gen AI at warp speed. Gen AI is the unstoppable wave transforming everything in its path. Comprehending its impact is not just optional; it's core to your survival in the corporate world. Second, ruthlessly evaluate your skills and expertise. Are they truly future-fit? If not, use the breather to **upskill or reskill**.

Let go of your ego. Expect to manage smaller teams in the future. The boast of "500 people work in my department" is passé. Expect more peers and fewer subordinates. People skills will skyrocket in importance; more on this in the 'IQ: for whom the bells toll' trend.

Lastly, remain conscious that the slight respite you have is just that—slight. This is a **temporary phase** until you embark on a similar journey as the junior and mid levels of your organization.

Finally, irrespective of which tier of the hierarchy you reside in, you need to confront two realities:

- The era of undertaking a single specialist role throughout your entire professional life is over. With technologies evolving and companies discovering novel ways to leverage them, job descriptions will morph rapidly—at least over the next ten years. Be prepared to reinvent yourself every few years. Say hello to squiggly careers!

- Star performers and hard-hitters—prepare to eat humble pie. The skill requirements of tomorrow are vastly different from those of yesteryears. As a result, many high and low performers will see a potential flip.

CHAPTER 3

THE FALL AND RISE OF SMALL BUSINESSES

Generative AI took command,
Innovation spread across the land.
Small businesses thrived,
From the fall, they revived,
Now they flourish, ideas grand.

– ChatGPT, on being prompted to "create a limerick on generative artificial intelligence and the fall & rise of small businesses"[1]

---

1   Created and retrieved on 26 May 2024

> *Small and many medium enterprises face an imminent short-term decline on the back of two tempests: inadequate resources to leverage Gen AI and the rise of the new-age conglomerate. Over time, the steep costs, resource constraints, accessibility challenges and other barriers required to ride the Gen AI wave will erode. Furthermore, enterprises will also adapt to the emergence of the new-age conglomerate. These tailwinds will stimulate the resurgence of small and mid-sized businesses.*

THE RATIONALE
GEN AI: THE AETHER

Can you imagine any decent-sized business today not using a computer, or some version of it? From design studios to cement manufacturing plants, from retail stores to coal mining — whether for storing and tracking data, connecting with customers and vendors, performing complex analytics, or controlling automated machines — the staggering range of users and applications all point to one conclusion: computers are indispensable.

In the years to come, Generative AI, along with its parent AI, will become the aether[2] — the all-pervasive substance once believed, until the 19th century, to fill space — infusing organizations as universally as computers and phones do today. Its potential to enrich capabilities, electrify efficiency,

---

2   Also spelt as 'ether'

and heighten returns across functions and throughout the product or service lifecycle renders Gen AI invaluable.

Starting with concept development: Gen AI spurs innovative ideas by analyzing mind-boggling volumes of data — market trends, customer preferences, substitute product sales, and more — to identify patterns. These patterns, in turn, act as fodder for Gen AI to craft new concepts and archetypes for potential customer offerings. The resulting concepts can be used as-is or refined through human ingenuity.

Concept frozen, Gen AI enables rapid progress through the product development process: designing, prototyping, validating, and testing. Combined with deep technologies such as Extended Reality (an umbrella term for immersive technologies including virtual reality, augmented reality, and mixed reality) and digital twinning (a digital or virtual replica of physical assets, processes, and systems), Gen AI exponentially accelerates the product development stage while reducing costs. No longer a need to physically manufacture hundreds of sample pieces to test for relevant parameters. Technology highlights defects and initiates 'virtual redesign and manufacturing' of a fresh batch for the next testing cycle. Depending on the complexity of the product, the end-to-end process can now take just a few hours to days — a sharp contrast to the weeks, or even months, required earlier for each cycle of physical production, testing, and redesign. The result: steep reductions in both time and investment.

Reaching the customer with the right message, at the right time, through the right medium characterizes an effective communication strategy. Big data analytics, combined with the pattern-creation prowess of Gen AI, ensures tailored communication for each recipient. Automated customization allows refinements in line with the nuance required for every individual customer — eliminating the tedious task of manually rewriting each variant. Dissecting historical recordings of customer calls — for word choices, voice tone, and other language attributes — enables Gen AI to tweak interactions accordingly. Needless to say, the outcome is spot-on. Companies such as Carrefour — the French retail and wholesale chain — have launched personalized shopping chatbots (Hopla, in this case) that factor in a shopper's budget and dietary restrictions when making purchase recommendations.[3] Fundamentally, Gen AI permits hyper-personalization of the customer experience (discussed in a later chapter).

Another spin-off application stems from Gen AI's generative abilities. Marketing blogs or articles that once took two to three days to research and write can now be created within minutes. Each refined version, thereafter, is churned out by Gen AI in a similar timeframe, compared to a few hours (at the least) by humans.

Collating data and drawing insights is another critical sphere of business operations. Gen AI facilitates the democratization of intelligent analytics and decision-

---

[3] 'Carrefour integrates OpenAI technologies and launches a generative AI-powered shopping experience', Carrefour website, 8 June 2023, Carrefour integrates OpenAI technologies and launches a generative AI-powered shopping experience | Carrefour Group

making. By analysing vast quantities of conventionally discrete data — whether customer research, sales, production, or finance-related — the system develops patterns, generates forecasts, and subsequently recommends an appropriate course of action.

Illustrative outputs include: What is the expected demand over the next three years, broken down by month, customer type, geography, brand, and myriad other parameters? What are the likely manufacturing defects, and how can they be fixed? What routes and warehouses should be used to optimise logistics and inventory, based on demand and production plants? Are there any red flags in the finances?

Depending on the 'human owner's' preference, Gen AI is even capable of initiating proactive action — for instance, identifying the need for predictive maintenance and proactively scheduling a maintenance appointment.

Gen AI ensures that advanced data analytics is available to all (democratisation) and, importantly, that the outputs are comprehensible to all — a concept often termed 'self-service business intelligence.'

MSMEs AND THE HARSH REALITY

From its transformational impact on internal operations to its game-changing effect on market-facing activities, the above-described use cases are merely the tip of the iceberg. Newer applications continue to be discovered. What is clear is that firms choosing to sit out the Gen AI wave will fail. Limited innovation, slower and costlier product development, an inability to strike a chord with existing and potential customers, and relatively inefficient production and distribution — these are just a few drivers of organizational collapse. Companies choosing to be technology-averse or opting not to adopt Gen AI for other reasons will turn uncompetitive, thereby marking their 'fall.'

Sadly, the harsh reality is that many firms — an overwhelming majority, in fact — in India are unable to adopt deep technologies and Gen AI in their full grandeur. Extensive resource requirements make adoption of AI and Gen AI implausible, at this stage, for MSMEs (micro, small, and medium enterprises), presenting a grave challenge for India due to three reasons: the prevalence of MSMEs, their contribution to the economy, and their role as an employment engine.

India: MSME land

India hosts 63.4 million MSMEs[4], accounting for well over 95 per cent[5] (over 98 per cent according to some estimates) of the total companies in India. Micro enterprises — defined as those having investment in plant, machinery, or equipment of not more than ₹1 crore and annual turnover of not more than ₹5 crore[6] — comprise more than 99 per cent (63.1 million enterprises) of the MSMEs. Medium enterprises — defined

---

4 'Estimated Number of MSMEs', Annual Report 2022 – 23, Ministry of Micro, Small and Medium Enterprises, MSMEANNUALREPORT2022-23ENGLISH.pdf

5 Precise statistics are unavailable due to parameters such as active and non-active companies

6 'What's MSME', Ministry of Micro, Small and Medium Enterprises website, What's MSME | Ministry of Micro, Small & Medium Enterprises

as those having investment in plant, machinery, or equipment of not more than ₹50 crore and annual turnover of not more than ₹250 crore[7] — number around 5,000 firms[8]. This split between micro, small, and medium enterprises is important in gauging the number of companies that will struggle to leverage Gen AI due to the investment involved.

MSMEs: the growth engine

MSMEs contributed 29.2 per cent[9] to India's overall GDP and 36.2 per cent[10] of its manufacturing output. While the share of MSME exports has been decreasing over time, it still remains a substantial 43.6 per cent.[11] Clearly, an uncompetitive MSME sector would be catastrophic for the country.

---

7 'What's MSME', Ministry of Micro, Small and Medium Enterprises website, What's MSME | Ministry of Micro, Small & Medium Enterprises

8 'Distribution of Enterprises Category Wise', Annual Report 2022 – 23, Ministry of Micro, Small and Medium Enterprises, MSMEANNUALREPORT2022-23ENGLISH.pdf

9 Figure for 2021-22, 'Role of MSME Sector in the Country', Ministry of Micro, Small & Medium Enterprises (PIB release), 7 August 2023, pib.gov.in/PressReleaseIframePage.aspx?PRID=1946375

10 Figure for 2021-22, 'Role of MSME Sector in the Country', Ministry of Micro, Small & Medium Enterprises (PIB release), 7 August 2023, pib.gov.in/PressReleaseIframePage.aspx?PRID=1946375

11 Figure for 2022-23, 'Role of MSME Sector in the Country', Ministry of Micro, Small & Medium Enterprises (PIB release), 7 August 2023, pib.gov.in/PressReleaseIframePage.aspx?PRID=1946375

From a sectoral perspective, MSMEs are roughly equally divided between trade (36 per cent of the total MSMEs), other services (33 per cent), and manufacturing (31 per cent) — negating the assumption that manufacturing will be hit harder than services.

MSMEs: keeping Indians employed

Employing a colossal 110 million people[12], MSMEs are the oxygen of the Indian economy, reiterating the criticality of prioritizing this segment of the corporate world.

Does Gen AI spell doom and the end of the MSME sector in India? Understanding the resources involved helps answer the question.

MODES OF LEVERAGING GEN AI

A brief recap before diving into the various modes for leveraging Gen AI. As the name suggests, generating content — text, images, video, audio, programming code — is its distinctive strength. Gen AI's ability to process and interact in natural language (the language you and I use, not complex software code) makes it especially valuable. Enabling human-language communication requires training systems on gigantic datasets (termed 'Large Language Models' or LLMs). For instance, OpenAI's GPT-3 model comprises 175

---

[12] 'Estimated Employment in the MSME Sector', Annual Report 2022 – 23, Ministry of Micro, Small and Medium Enterprises, MSMEANNUALREPORT2022-23ENGLISH.pdf

billion parameters,[13] while AI21 Labs' Jurassic-1 model has 178 billion parameters.[14]

To clarify, Gen AI is more than just text, both from an input and output perspective. LLMs are a key component of Gen AI systems, but by no means the only ones. Other common components include image creation, video generation, music composition, and more.

Broadly, there are three modes for organizations to leverage Gen AI: build, adapt, or use as-is.

1. Build
Traditional Large Language Models

Developing and training a traditional Large Language Model (LLM) is exorbitantly expensive, even for a mega international corporation. While precise figures are not publicly available, Sam Altman — OpenAI's founder — famously responded "more than that" at an MIT event when asked whether OpenAI spent USD 100 million on GPT.[15] Experts forecast that the next generation of LLMs will

---

13 'What are Large Language Models (LLM)?' AWS website, What are Large Language Models? - LLM AI Explained - AWS (amazon.com)

14 'Announcing AI21 Studio and Jurassic-1 language models', AI21 website, Announcing AI21 Studio and Jurassic-1 language models

15 'What Large Models Cost You – There Is No Free AI Lunch', Forbes, 8 September 2023, What Large Models Cost You – There Is No Free AI Lunch (forbes.com)

cost upwards of USD 1 billion,[16] despite cost-containment strategies like quantum computing.

Multiple factors drive these sky-high costs. Gigantic and the continuously growing size of training datasets means longer training times and more iterations, leading to enormous computational power and electricity requirements. Processing at this scale demands thousands of Graphics Processing Units (GPUs) operating in parallel, with the training process stretching over several months.

Even the query-handling stage is a major resource drain, necessitating full-fledged data centers. One estimate suggests that ChatGPT used over 30,000 GPUs, consuming 1 Gigawatt hour (GWh) daily in January 2023 to handle user requests. To put that into perspective: assuming an urban Indian household consumes 200 KWh per month (the amount of free electricity provided by the Delhi government), 1 GWh per day equals the daily power usage of 150,000 Indian households.

Given the astronomical costs involved — multiples of the annual turnover of Indian MSMEs — building an in-house LLM, and thus a Gen AI system, is not a viable option. From a core competency perspective as well, developing cutting-edge technology is best left to technology companies, while other firms should focus on leveraging these applications to achieve their strategic goals. With several LLMs already available — GPT-4 (OpenAI), Claude (Anthropic), Bard (Google),

---

16 'What Large Models Cost You – There Is No Free AI Lunch', Forbes, 8 September 2023, What Large Models Cost You – There Is No Free AI Lunch (forbes.com)

LLaMA (Meta), Chinchilla (DeepMind) — and more on the horizon, the imperative for any single organization to develop its own LLM is low.

Small Language Models

An alternative approach is to build a scaled-down or skeletal version of an LLM, known as a Small Language Model (SLM). There is no strict demarcation between 'large' and 'small,' though some consider models under 100 million parameters as 'small,' while others set the threshold as low as 1 million. As the number of parameters decreases, evaluating the model's capabilities and accuracy becomes especially critical. SLMs are typically designed for simpler tasks and are often domain-specific.

The cost structure for building and operating an SLM mirrors that of an LLM — albeit on a much smaller scale, depending on the size and desired capability of the model. While this could place SLM development within the reach of large corporates, the technology is still evolving. For MSMEs, investing crores of rupees into building an SLM that could become obsolete within two to four years is both foolhardy and financially unsound.

Moreover, the 'non-core business' argument, similar to that for LLMs, persists. As a rough analogy — would it be sensible for a ₹20 crore turnover auto-component manufacturer to invest in building an accounting software? Or for a salon clocking around ₹2 crore revenue a year to develop its proprietary UPI system?

The disruptive Gen AI system

Come early 2025, enter DeepSeek — annihilating conventional Gen AI thinking in four fundamental ways: architecture, training pedagogy, GPUs, and access.

In contrast to traditional Gen AI systems, DeepSeek employs a Mixture-of-Experts (MoE) architecture. Think of MoE as breaking a single gigantic committee into multiple smaller expert teams. Instead of mobilizing all members of the committee for every request, DeepSeek activates only the relevant 'expert team' — a sub-set of its 671 billion parameters. Traditional models such as ChatGPT, in contrast, fire up all parameters simultaneously, following an 'all-hands-on-deck' approach. Selective activation drastically reduces computation needs and processing costs, while also enabling DeepSeek to deliver results faster, boosting efficiency for specific tasks.

Until now, Gen AI systems have primarily used supervised learning — training algorithms on labelled datasets and relying on instruction-based fine-tuning, which requires extensive human intervention. Vast teams of humans review the responses for accuracy, driving up both time and cost. DeepSeek upends this model by automating much of the process using reinforcement learning. Instead of depending on manual reviews, the system learns from experience and self-corrects to maximise performance-based rewards. The result: significantly lower development timelines, and cheaper, more scalable models.

A major expense for Gen AI models is the chips that power them — the Graphics Processing Units (GPUs). Legacy systems typically operate on high-performance but expensive and supply-constrained H100 and A100 chips. DeepSeek's disruptive edge stems not only from its unconventional GPU choice but also its design. Using Nvidia's less powerful, more readily available H800 GPUs enables substantial cost reduction. Further, by opting for a PTX (Parallel Thread Execution) architecture — a programming model that splits vast amounts of data into smaller parts for parallel processing — DeepSeek is able to squeeze more performance out of the mid-tier H800 GPUs, while also speeding up computations.

Beyond its technical innovations, DeepSeek has also disrupted the prevailing business model. Most traditional AI models are proprietary — their code, training data, and methodologies remain closed, with limited access offered to paying customers via APIs. DeepSeek changes the rules of play by democratizing access. As an open-source system, its code, architecture, and weights are publicly available — allowing anyone to fine-tune and deploy the model for their own applications.

The verdict

DeepSeek overturns the conventional Gen AI cost–performance equation, slashing both development and usage costs while still delivering high performance for technical tasks. Contrast the billions of dollars spent on developing traditional Gen AI systems with the USD 6 million spent on DeepSeek. The economics don't stop there — usage costs, measured by token pricing, are also around 27 times cheaper.

Designed for efficient processing, DeepSeek's Mixture-of-Experts architecture makes it a powerhouse for coding and complex mathematical problem-solving. On the flip side, triggering all parameters simultaneously allows legacy systems to outperform DeepSeek in terms of versatility. General-purpose reasoning, knowledge-based queries, creativity, conversational flow, and storytelling remain the stronghold of traditional Gen AI models.

In conclusion, the moot question remains: should (non-technology) MSMEs invest in building a DeepSeek equivalent? The rationale against building a SLM — a risky, non-core business investment — applies here too.

2. Adapt
Large Language Models

An alternative to building an in-house Gen AI system is fine-tuning existing LLMs, which involves adapting the pre-trained LLM to your specific needs. This entails further training the model using targeted datasets. For example, the off-the-shelf LLM can identify birds, perhaps even a kingfisher. However, birdwatchers would want to know whether they spotted a collared kingfisher, pied kingfisher, azure kingfisher, or other variants. Fine-tuning the LLM to include this functionality would achieve that.

Training an LLM involves collecting, cleaning, and preparing the dataset. Larger LLMs, being more sophisticated, require smaller datasets for specific use cases. 'Smaller' is a relative term; the models still need thousands or tens of thousands of examples, depending on the end goal. On the other hand, larger models require more computational power, meaning higher GPU requirements. One estimate suggests that the GPU setup cost for GPT-3 ranges between Rs 80 – 90 lakh. Leveraging cloud computing can convert the capital expenditure into operating expenses (estimated at Rs 2000 – 2100 per hour),[17] making Gen AI more accessible to MSMEs. Needless to say, AI development costs and time must be considered.

Fine-tuning an LLM involves an initial deployment cost, followed by recurring maintenance expenses. One assessment puts the one-time expense and maintenance cost at Rs 1.6 – 1.7 crore, with an annual maintenance expense of Rs 12 lakh.[18]

Operating expenses depend on the scale of usage. Once the system is set up, LLM companies charge a fee for running queries, adopting the quintessential pay-per-use model on a per-token basis (a token is approximately three-fourths of a word).

Small Language Models

Fine-tuning a SLM is another option for leveraging Gen AI for specific activities. With lower resource requirements—both in terms of cost and time—compared to fine-tuning an LLM, this approach may be more feasible for MSMEs. However, SLMs are trained on domain-specific data and have limited broader contextual knowledge. Fine-tuning an SLM further

---

17 'Evaluating the cost of generative AI for effective implementation in your organization', ITREX website, 21 December 2023, Calculating the Cost of Generative AI — ITRex (itrexgroup.com)

18 'Evaluating the cost of generative AI for effective implementation in your organization', ITREX website, 21 December 2023, Calculating the Cost of Generative AI — ITRex (itrexgroup.com)

narrows its scope of operations. From a cost perspective, the sum of multiple fine-tuned SLMs may end up being higher than a single multi-purpose fine-tuned LLM.

The verdict

Fine-tuning a Gen AI system, whether based on an LLM or SLM, appears to be within the affordability range for larger mid-sized Indian companies. However, the real challenge for MSMEs lies in the availability of high-quality in-house data. Fine-tuning a model to deliver accurate outputs hinges on access to a sufficient volume of labeled, robust training data. The optimal data size depends on the intended task, its complexity, and the specifications of the foundational model. Even fine-tuning an SLM for basic tasks requires a few hundred examples. Most large corporations in India struggle to assemble a dataset of this nature, let alone MSMEs. Without enough quality samples, the accuracy and reliability of the results are questionable. As the saying goes, "garbage in, garbage out!"

Buying datasets is a possibility; although the applicability of generic or set-in-other-context examples is questionable. In a sense, the outcome would be similar to the third mode to leverage Gen AI: use as-is.

3. Use as-is

At the other end of the spectrum is deploying existing off-the-shelf Gen AI systems, as-is, without any customization. An Application Programming Interface (API), which is a software intermediary that enables two discrete programs to communicate, facilitates integration of the chosen Gen

AI model into the organization's existing software systems, allowing employees to access it seamlessly.

The expenses and resource requirements for this mode are lower (but not zero) compared to the earlier two options. However, costs for adequate computational power (either in-house or via cloud computing), API development, integration, and electricity will need to be budgeted. Additionally, Gen AI models charge an access fee – pay per token – based on usage.

On the flip side, the lack of customization or fine-tuning the model results in generic responses. Off-the-shelf LLM or SLM-based models lack the contextual knowledge specific to your business, raising doubts about the utility of the output. This issue is even more pronounced due to the lack of SLMs focused on the Indian MSME sector, whose needs differ greatly from those of large corporations in India or mid-sized businesses in developed economies.

Over time, as more targeted SLMs enter the market, the effectiveness of using a non-customized model will improve. For now, each organization should conduct a thorough evaluation to determine the specific value delivered by the various Gen AI models.

THE RISE OF THE NEW-AGE CONGLOMERATE

Gen AI, either on its own or combined with other deep technologies, will push certain sectors toward redundancy. Think back to the 1990s or earlier. Postal services were a vital part of every country's infrastructure. Both individuals and businesses relied on and demanded an efficient, fast, and widespread postal network to ensure smooth communication.

Enter email. In less than a decade, postal services and their associated sectors shrivelled dramatically.

Gen AI is the 'email' of the 21st century. The ease of accomplishing certain tasks – literally with a keystroke – prompts organizations to in-source these activities. As a result, firms providing these services (as vendors) will shrink to a fraction of their current size or cease to exist. Take a software firm engaged in rudimentary programming. A request in conversational (non-programming) language by even a non-techie can get Gen AI to generate error-free code in seconds. Auto-generated code transforms the once valuable coding service provider into an expendable appendage, with no concrete role. When magnified at a sector level, programming firms, especially those handling elementary or non-complex outsourced work, will either wither or perish.

Low-end content generation firms face a similar fate. Gen AI can gather the necessary information and compose a high-quality draft of the organization's Annual Report, including messages from the Chair and Managing Director, all within minutes. Contrast this with the multiple-month timeframe required for a human-generated Annual Report.

On the advertising front, Gen AI can spawn multiple options for social media posts – whether text, images, or videos – along with blogs, articles, and other marketing materials, within seconds. Based on an analysis of the target audience, Gen AI can even recommend the most appropriate option, with more scientific rigor than humans. Similar examples abound, all pointing to the potential extinction of certain sub-sectors as independent business opportunities.

As end-user companies increase their adoption of Gen AI, they will find that many tasks, such as those mentioned earlier, can be undertaken internally with no additional resources. In fact, in-house execution may prove cheaper and more efficient. A throwback to the early 20th-century vertically integrated corporations – but with a Gen AI twist. Ergo, the rise of the new-age conglomerate.

Firms in affected or 'victim' sectors, regardless of their size, will shrink and eventually fade away. Larger or well-funded firms could channelize their resources to pivot into other businesses or sustain themselves until they do. Smaller firms will likely struggle with the transition. Unlike past seismic shifts (such as the decline of music CDs), which were gradual and allowed time for reinvention, Gen AI is moving at hyper-speed, further compounding the challenge.

GEN AI AND MSMEs: TRACKING THEIR TRAJECTORY
The downfall of MSMEs ...

Synthesizing the implications of the modes through which organizations can harness Gen AI indicates the likely adoption trajectory for MSMEs in India. In the short term, MSMEs will grapple with one or a combination of high costs, resource constraints (such as high-quality data), and limited appropriate off-the-shelf products. The consequence: curbing of their ability to fully wield the power of Gen AI, preventing the firms from capitalizing on the enhanced capabilities and returns (a few illustrations of which were provided earlier in this chapter) that the technology enables.

An argument could be made that DeepSeek eliminates the hurdles for adoption of Gen AI by MSMEs. While the cost barrier has certainly crashed, four formidable impediments persist: relevance, data, contextualization, and accessibility.

As mentioned earlier, DeepSeek excels in coding and complex mathematical tasks, capabilities of limited relevance to most MSMEs. A more fundamental challenge is the non-availability of high-quality data. Purchasing data may appear to be a workaround, but it is not. Contextualization, or incorporating the nuances of the specific business environment, comes into play: the smaller the firm, the more critical hyper-localized data is for training AI systems. Outputs derived from European or US-centric data are of little value to small firms operating in the vastly different Indian environment. A similar line of reasoning applies to DeepSeek and its successors (referred to as 'DeepSeek equivalents'). Accessibility poses the fourth challenge. Currently, most Gen AI systems operate in English. Until they are available in regional Indian languages, accessibility will remain a constraint for MSMEs. Over time, these barriers will ease, with DeepSeek equivalents accelerating the process. For now, though, the obstacles persist.

In contrast, larger firms will scale the competitiveness ladder with Gen AI. In their case, the challenges MSMEs face in adopting Gen AI are largely mitigated by deep pockets and institutionalized processes.

Picture this: larger corporations ascending the competitiveness ladder—rapidly and often in game-changing ways—while MSMEs remain stagnant. The resulting widening gap threatens the survival of MSMEs. Aggravating the situation is the rise of the new-age conglomerates, where large companies bring outsourced activities in-house. Small enterprises dependent on outsourcing by these large firms may dwindle or vanish as the latter absorb these activities internally. There are, however, a few notable exceptions in the MSME cohort, which are discussed later.

... and their resurgence

At the same time, tailwinds in the form of reducing investment, a larger basket of available products, and innovative business models signal the rise of the phoenix.

As with all technologies, over time, the costs associated with traditional Gen AI systems will fall. Expanding the user base enables Gen AI firms to spread their expenses over a larger number of customers, reducing per-user charges. Furthermore, technologies like GPUs, cloud computing, and associated hardware are becoming cheaper, along with declining premiums charged by AI developers.

The mobile app marketplace is now flooded with products catering to a diverse range of customer profiles and niche applications. Similarly, growing demand will spur the proliferation of newer Gen AI systems, allowing small businesses to adopt off-the-shelf products with limited or no fine-tuning, and at greater efficacy. Affordable access to relevant products will drive Gen AI adoption among MSMEs, enabling the sector to regain its market power.

Another element with the potential to elevate the competitiveness of small businesses is innovative business models and strategies. Software as a Service (SaaS)—cloud-based delivery of application software by a third-party provider who also manages the physical and software resources used by the application—is already a familiar concept in the technology sector. Users benefit by converting capital expenditure into operational costs, ensuring that smaller users can still access expensive technologies. A similar "AI as a Service" (AIaaS) model is beginning to take root. Complementing the emergence of new business models externally, smarter MSMEs in victim sectors will also devise ways to survive the rise of new-age conglomerates, by pivoting into other areas or offering value adds that differentiate their services from Gen AI.

THE OUTLIERS

Although grouped together as one category, MSMEs are an immensely heterogeneous group: micro organizations are vastly different from mid-sized firms, and small companies differ from micro enterprises. This is unsurprising, given the elephantine range of revenues (from negligible to Rs 250 crore) and capital investment (from negligible to Rs 50 crore) covered under the MSME definition.[19] In fact, distinctive cohorts can be identified even within a category (e.g., mid-sized companies).

In this context, a few clusters of enterprises will buck the U-shaped trend of the downfall and rise of MSMEs.

---

19 'What's MSME', Ministry of Micro, Small and Medium Enterprises website, What's MSME | Ministry of Micro, Small & Medium Enterprises

1. The giant 'M's

Medium enterprises are defined by a combination of turnover and fixed assets investment. The turnover range is wide: from Rs 50 crore to 250 crore, while the capital investment limit is set at Rs 50 crore.

Most service firms do not invest in plant and machinery; the Rs 50 crore ceiling could well cover the assets investment of large service companies. The turnover criterion is, therefore, relevant for services firms. Companies at the higher end of the spectrum are significantly more sophisticated than those at the lower end—a distinction further amplified by the fact that the turnover threshold does not include export revenues.[20] Thus, firms at the upper end of the band are likely to be larger than the average Rs 250 crore organization and will exhibit even higher levels of maturity.

For manufacturing firms, on the other hand, the Rs 50 crore limit for plant and machinery is relatively low, depending on the specific sub-sector, indicating a lower level of sophistication.

Mature organizations, typically larger mid-sized companies, have easier access to funding—either from internal reserves or externally—as well as more rigorous data and processes in place to comprehensively integrate Gen AI into their operations. As a result, these sophisticated mid-sized organizations should be able to ride the first wave of Gen AI and counter the downward trend.

---

20 'What is the definition of MSME', Ministry of Micro, Small and Medium Enterprises website, Q.1. What is the definition of MSME | Ministry of Micro, Small & Medium Enterprises

2. Star start-ups

Well-funded start-ups, flush with venture capital or private equity investment, are another category of organizations that will resist the fall. These firms, from inception, tend to be technologically savvy and embrace new-age systems that can integrate with Gen AI. Investors, too, are generally open to infusing additional money to escalate their ventures up the technology curve.

Needless to say, AI and deep-tech firms, in general, will be exceptions to the trend of small enterprises being quashed.

3. Below the radar micros

(Please note, 'star start-ups' as mentioned in point #2 above are exceptions to the impact described in this section.)

Micro enterprises, in themselves, are an ocean, spanning an assortment of sectors and sizes. From food processing to power looms to auto ancillary, they encompass diverse manufacturing sub-sectors. Similarly, micro enterprises are the backbone of the Indian services industry—beauty parlours, coaching classes, and catering, to name a few.

An estimated 66 per cent to 95 per cent of micro firms have a turnover under Rs 50 lakh, with 45 per cent to 89 per cent reporting revenues under Rs 12 lakh.[21] Regardless of the precise figures, it is safe to say that an overwhelming

---

21 The 95 per cent and 89 per cent figures are basis National Sample Survey of Organizations, while the 66 per cent and 45 per cent figures are basis Annual Survey of Industries. Figures quoted in 'The Course of Smallness', The Indian Express, 20 May 2024, MSMEs have not been defined well — and micro enterprises pay the price for this | The Indian Express

majority of these firms operate with low turnover and, thus, register low profit margins (in absolute terms). From a Gen AI perspective, in addition to affordability issues, their level of technology adoption is generally low. In fact, efforts are ongoing to kick-start their journey on the digitalization curve, starting at rudimentary levels. Clearly, this cohort is a long way from adopting Gen AI.

Micro enterprises typically serve customers distinct from those targeted by large or medium-sized companies. Over the next few years, the more sophisticated firms are unlikely to vie for the customers of micro enterprises. For instance, a mid-sized packaging company would aim to capture business from similarly sized or larger consumer goods companies, not produce carry bags from used newspapers for roadside food vendors. Further, most micro enterprises compete with other micro firms, not large or medium-sized companies.

It is for these reasons that a large proportion of micro enterprises will buck the trend of turning uncompetitive in the short term.

JUMP-STARTING YOUR COMPANY

If you are a small or mid-sized company that doesn't qualify in one of the outlier categories, should you shut shop and run? Absolutely not. Use the seven pointers below to thrive.

1. Gauge your sophistication score

Evaluate your organization's readiness to adopt Gen AI. Conduct a thorough assessment of the resources available, including access to funding (whether internal or external), data availability, and other enablers. A vital catalyst is a mentally prepared and trained employee base. An honest appraisal will help your company select the optimal execution strategy.

Keep in mind that organizations evolve over time; your company may rate low on the sophistication scale today, but with intense efforts, you may propel it to a high score in a year. Your Gen AI approach should evolve accordingly.

2. Select a Gen AI execution approach

Map your company's sophistication score to the resource requirements of various modes of leveraging Gen AI. This will help determine the optimal execution strategy. At the same time, keep an eye on your competitors: What are they doing? How are they overcoming the challenge of inadequate, high-quality in-house data, if this is the case? Integrating Gen AI is a pivotal strategic decision—probably the most critical of the decade. Your company's best minds should be involved in formulating the roadmap.

3. Garner ammunition

A large proportion of firms in India, including many large companies, lack an adequate quantum of high-quality in-house data for training models. Purchasing data is the obvious workaround, though it may only be a temporary solution depending on your specific needs.

At the same time, establish processes and systems to build your in-house data arsenal on a war footing. The results from fine-tuning Gen AI models with in-house contextual data are far superior to those using generic data. Start by identifying the information you need and prioritizing high-impact, easy wins (unless your organization can handle multiple fronts!).

4. Together, we rise

The most powerful strategy for a David to compete with Goliath is to join forces with other Davids—classic coopetition, or cooperating while competing. Many small and medium enterprises lack the data and technical resources required to adopt Gen AI, despite funding not being a roadblock for some.

Innovative business models and progressive mindsets are key. Pooling resources, particularly data, can help overcome these challenges. A shared data set, for example, could be used to fine-tune an existing model. Although the outcome may not be perfect given the training data isn't bespoke for each company, it will give firms a valuable head start. Instead of an entire cohort of companies struggling to compete, joining forces allows them to play in the big league.

5. Demand aggregation - the superpower

The ideal scenario for all organizations, particularly those at the middle or lower end of the sophistication scale, is a plethora of relevant off-the-shelf Gen AI models that require little to no fine-tuning. A single firm prodding developers to focus on a specific sector or market segment is unlikely to spark action. On the other hand, a group of companies expressing interest in a product excites IT firms. Transforming a lone potential customer into a collective group of potential customers makes it worthwhile for developers to create and market the new product.

Adopting a similar 'team approach' would also benefit larger, more sophisticated companies. The more appropriate a product, the less customization is needed, which lowers the cost and accelerates execution.

6. Guerrilla warfare for survival

Is your company in a victim sector? Scrutinize your business clinically; the tendency is to overstate the value your company adds to customers. Can Gen AI deliver the same, or perhaps even better, outputs? The technology is still nascent, and capabilities are being enhanced weekly, so be cautious in your assessment. Incipiency implies that the assessment should be carried out periodically; what might seem like an unaffected sector today could slip into the victim sector bucket in six months.

If the answer to the original question is yes, your company is in a victim sector or likely to be in one—whether large or small—an urgent strategy refresh is needed. The two routes for survival are pivot or adapt. Transition out of your current business focus to one that builds on your company's capabilities and strengths. Alternatively, hold steadfast in the same area, but review your offering. Can you enhance the value delivered to customers with an add-on that Gen AI cannot provide? Consider the travel industry as an analogy. The advent of online platforms allowed travelers to book flights, hotels, and transportation with ease from the comfort of their homes. Travel agents became redundant, and their business was decimated. Few shut shop, and few took on fledgling businesses. But the ones who thrive offer additional benefits, such as curating luxury tours or adventure trips.

Guerrilla warfare at its best: avoid head-on confrontation, find weak spots, and flank the competitor (Gen AI, in this case).

7. Elicit support

Integrating Gen AI is resource-heavy—requiring funding, computational power, and expertise—and demands concurrent initiatives on multiple fronts. Frequently, these prerequisites may be out of reach for many MSMEs, including your company.

Seek government assistance, whether in the form of subsidized funding, knowledge-building sessions, or common data pools. Driving MSMEs up the digitalization curve is central to the Government of India's agenda, as seen in programs like Digital India and the IndiaAI mission. Supporting MSMEs in their Gen AI journey aligns with the government's overall vision.

JUMP-STARTING YOUR CAREER

While this mega-trend pertains to the evolving industry structures and their organizational ramifications, there are actions you, as an individual employee, can take to future-proof your career.

1. Trust, but verify

"Doverey, no proverey," as the Russian proverb goes: trust, but verify. Assess your company's position on the sophistication scale to determine the optimal mode of integrating Gen AI into operations.

Simultaneously, evaluate whether your company falls into a victim sector. To recap, many industries will rapidly pivot from being Gen AI-tenacious to victim sectors. Your company's leadership may have the organization's best interests in mind; however, top management often leans towards groupthink and an echo chamber of over-optimism about the resilience of the company's business.

A realistic assessment of your company's state, combined with the response of top brass, will steer your course of action.

2. Spur action

Provoke action within your company. The tight timeframes for Gen AI impact demand quick planning and rapid execution. Organizations often miss this imperative in their desire to develop a perfect, foolproof plan. Moreover, progressive mindsets, such as collaborating with competitors, can be difficult and alien concepts for your company's leadership and others in the organization. Advocating for its value and urgency will help persuade the team.

3. Lead the effort

Become a Gen AI champion, both at the individual and organizational level. Discern its implications for your company, and based on your familiarity with AI, this may require some research. Take a leadership role in your organization. Keep in mind, this is a new discipline, so it's fair game for anyone who gets the ball rolling.

4. Jump ship: the last resort

In the rare—but not impossible—situation where your company's leadership is impervious to the repercussions of Gen AI and refuses to heed advice, it would be prudent to rethink your professional future. Exercise special caution if your company operates in a victim sector. In such cases, you may want to explore opportunities outside your current organization.

CHAPTER 4

THE WORLD REVOLVES AROUND YOU

There once was a bot quite wise,
Who crafted responses to size,
With AI so keen,
Hyper-personalized scene,
Left users in pleasant surprise.

– ChatGPT, on being prompted to "create a limerick on generative artificial intelligence and hyper-personalization"[1]

---

1 Created and retrieved on 14 June 2024

> *Hyper-personalization is the new mantra. Individualization pervades every aspect of the customer experience: from the product or service, to communication and after-sales service. Amongst the key ramifications are decentralization and localization of manufacturing, and the need for flexible manufacturing. Key elements of hyper-personalization are already being implemented. The weak link, which is rapidly being addressed, is weaving the components together to offer a seamless customized experience to the consumer.*

THE RATIONALE
HISTORY REPEATS ITSELF

Karl Marx's proclamation 'history repeats itself' - the opening lines of his essay 'The Eighteenth Brumaire of Louis Napoleon' published in Die Revolution (1852) – has proven to be profoundly prophetic. In a throwback to the pre-industrialization era, generally considered prior to 1750, firms of the future will serve each customer as an unique individual, catering to his or her distinct preferences and tastes.

Lack of machines and mass production capabilities characterized the pre-industrialization age. Clothes were stitched on a bespoke basis or in very small batches, which could then be altered for each customer. Chefs baked bread tailored to local palates. In modern parlance, this was "product customization."

In contrast, the Gen AI epoch offers the optionality of hyper-personalized customer experiences. Organizations can now group customers into small, largely homogeneous segments and cater to their specific affinities. These segments will wither — eventually collapsing into a segment of one — as Gen AI grows increasingly powerful.

Today, mega-factories churn out millions of pieces of apparel and loaves of bread using standardized designs and recipes. If your only request is blue buttons instead of white, or slightly fewer sesame seeds on a sourdough you otherwise love, you're out of luck — you have to settle for the default version. Gen AI is dispelling that reality, and is already well on its way to erasing it altogether.

THE HYPER-PERSONAL CUSTOMER EXPERIENCE

Building a composite profile of you — the potential customer — is the foundation for delivering a hyper-personalized customer journey. Gen AI processes and analyzes a multitude of traditionally discrete datasets: your historical choices in clothing, music, groceries, books, movies, vacations, interests, financial state, and countless other data points. Patterns emerge, creating a detailed image of who you are — your likes, dislikes, preferences, and ambitions. Perhaps even more than you consciously know about yourself.

Curate a bespoke offering for you

An apparel brand's Gen AI system dissects your profile to understand your preferences in attire (Indian vs. Western), style (classic vs. trendy), material (organic sustainable vs. conventional; cotton vs. silk), colour, budget, and size — among hundreds (or even thousands) of other variables. The output, combined with Gen AI's generative capabilities, is an apparel design ideally suited to your taste and budget.

Ditto for bread. Your data reveals preferences for crust (hard vs. soft), taste (sweetness of wheat vs. tanginess of rye), loaf size (do you live alone or with family? how often do you eat bread?), allergies (gluten-free, nut-free), add-ons (onion vs. cheese), and more. These insights blend to generate your perfect loaf.

Accessing your soft corners

Product personalized, next step: enticing you to buy it — and ensuring it's easy to access. Your psychographic profile guides the development of a communication strategy: the what, how, and where of the message. Variables like your preference for message type (factual vs. emotional), tonality (humorous vs. serious), appeal (cute dogs vs. serene landscapes), influencers (Bollywood stars, athletes, relatable everyday people), and the publications you read, all help shape a communication plan crafted just for you.

Your habits also determine how best to deliver the product to you. Are you an in-store shopper or an online buyer? Which physical or digital places do you frequent?

Always there for you

Post-sale customer service is the cornerstone for spawning repeat customers. By analyzing your psychographic profile – the tonality of voice, idioms, etc. you are inclined to – companies can transform a forgettable interaction into a delightful memory.

Circularity for you

Gen AI predicts when you're likely to be ready for your next purchase, allowing companies to proactively reach you at the right time. And with the option of recycling if you're tagged as a sustainability advocate.

And so, welcome to the you-centric world

The 'you-centric world' is not as fantastical as it appears. For centuries, astronomers considered Earth to be at the center of the universe. Eudoxus, a Greek mathematician and astronomer, created the 'geometric geocentric model' around 380 BC,[2] placing Earth at the core, surrounded by 27 concentric spheres containing the Sun, Moon, and stars. Science legends like Callippus, Aristotle, and Ptolemy refined the framework. It took nearly two thousand years for this belief to be replaced by the heliocentric model introduced by Copernicus in the 1500s. The idea gained further support with Galileo's work in the 1600s.[3]

Echoing earlier astronomers, Gen AI revives the notion of the individual as the locus of life (philosophically, of course, not astronomically!).

---

2 'Eudoxus of Cnidus', Britannica, Eudoxus of Cnidus | Greek Mathematician, Astronomer & Philosopher | Britannica

3 'History of astronomy', Britannica, 17 June 2024, Astronomy - Ancient, Celestial, Observations | Britannica; 'A Brief History', Observational Cosmology, University of Wisconsin – Madison, Department of Physics, Brief History (wisc.edu)

HYPER-PERSONALIZATION: SCI-FI FOR NOW?

Is hyper-personalization a distant reality, an ingredient for science fiction? An emphatic no. Many elements of the puzzle are already in place, and the final link is rapidly coming together.

Hyper-personalized messaging and marketing

From an execution perspective, customized messaging is a relatively low-hanging (nothing in AI is 'simple,' but relatively 'simple' due to multiple existing use-cases!) yet effective win. Starbucks combines a customer's drink preference, past purchases, and other activity with real-time data to send unique personalized offers. The coffee giant's AI engine generates over 400,000 variations of hyper-personalized messages.[4] Secret Escapes adapts its website based on search keywords or the ad you clicked on. For instance, if you type 'luxury spa resorts,' the landing page tailors its images and text to match. Estimates suggest Secret Escapes witnessed a 26 per cent increase in sign-ups due to personalization.[5]

Moving beyond messaging, companies are now explicitly recommending specific products to customers. TastryAI partners with wineries and wine retailers to suggest wines

---

4 'The 20 Most Compelling Examples Of Personalization', Forbes, 29 March 2021, The 20 Most Compelling Examples Of Personalization (forbes.com)

5 '10 examples of hyper-personalized marketing', Wedia, 19 October 2022, 10 examples of hyper-personalized marketing (wedia-group.com)

to a consumer by mapping their palate. A 20-second quiz, featuring questions such as 'your reaction to the smell of fresh-cut grass,' is all the TastryAI system needs to identify compounds you like or dislike, and consequently the wines you're likely to enjoy. Closing the loop, based on customer feedback on the recommended wines, the AI system fine-tunes future recommendations.[6]

Threads, an online fashion retailer, uses an AI algorithm to propose products based on your preferred styles, body type, budget, and feedback on previous purchases. Perry Ellis, the men's fashion brand, offers a similar service.[7] CoverGirl, a cosmetics brand, integrates augmented reality with individualized recommendations based on skin tone and facial features, allowing customers to 'see' the effect of the suggestions on themselves.[8] Custom haircare brand Prose goes a step further by creating a personalized product, complete with the consumer's name on the bottle.[9]

Amazon is among the most sophisticated users of hyper-personalized marketing. Have you opened the Amazon website or app and had that eerie feeling that the content

---

6 '10 examples of hyper-personalized marketing', Wedia, 19 October 2022, 10 examples of hyper-personalized marketing (wedia-group.com)

7 ibid

8 'The 20 Most Compelling Examples Of Personalization', Forbes, 29 March 2021, The 20 Most Compelling Examples Of Personalization (forbes.com)

9 '10 examples of hyper-personalized marketing', Wedia, 19 October 2022, 10 examples of hyper-personalized marketing (wedia-group.com)

almost perfectly matches your needs? That's because it does. Amazon mines your past history – purchases made, products searched, time spent, etc. – to run predictive analysis on your future buying behavior. Overlaying 'collaborative filtering,' that is, scanning the purchase history of other customers who have bought similar products, the company derives a list of 'frequently bought together' items. Amazon doesn't stop there. It also scrutinizes your browsing history to strengthen the robustness of the recommendation.[10] As a simple example, assume you bought a set of record-player (turntable) needles. The AI model also detects that you recently watched the movie 'Mamma Mia!' (the superhit film revolving around ABBA songs) on Prime Video. Linking the two together, Amazon recommends the 'Mamma Mia!' vinyl (or record, as it's also known).

Hyper-personalized production

Customized communication or marketing promises to be both impactful and relatively easier to execute. For manufacturers, however, the big question and potential stumbling block is whether new-age manufacturing technologies can produce customized batch sizes at an economically viable cost. In other words, is tailored production feasible? Additive manufacturing offers a solution and is being actively explored by both end-consumer-facing (business-to-consumer, or B2C) and non-facing (business-to-business, or B2B) firms.

Hershey's introduced a 3D candy printing machine at its Hershey's Chocolate World Attraction facility in the USA,

---

10 ibid

allowing visitors to 'print' their own unique chocolate bars.[11] The company expects to place these machines in all its retail stores soon. Gillette launched its Razor Maker platform, enabling customers to select customized shaver handle designs, which are then 3D printed.[12] Customers share photos of their feet with FitMyFoot, a custom insole and shoe company. A 3D digital map of each foot is created, with slight differences between the right and left feet also taken into account. Bespoke products, based on the customer's choice of design and color, are then produced.[13]

Another major user sector is dental and medical implants, including medical devices. Hip and dental prostheses are prime examples.[14] In an offbeat instance, Chanel 3D bioprinted skin with a pigment spot to assess the effectiveness of its skincare products.[15] The company has also been using

---

11 'Every home to have a 3-D printer sooner than you think, says Hershey', Confectionary News, 6 October 2021, 3D chocolate printing has bright future, says Hershey (confectionerynews.com)

12 '10 Companies (And Many More) That Already Use 3D Printing' Septillion, 23 September 2020, 10 Companies (And Many More) That Already Use 3D Printing (septillion.co.th)

13 'The 20 Most Compelling Examples Of Personalization', Forbes, 29 March 2021, The 20 Most Compelling Examples Of Personalization (forbes.com)

14 'What industries use 3D printing', Trumpf, **What industries use 3D printing | TRUMPF**

15 'Chanel Has Developed 3D Bioprinted Skin to Improve its Skincare Projects', 3D Natives, 27 February 2023, Chanel Has Developed 3D Bioprinted Skin to Improve its Skincare Projects - 3Dnatives

3D printing to create mascara brushes. Companies like Ford, Airbus, NASA, and SpaceX have been using additive manufacturing for years to print components.

Designing customized offerings by harnessing Gen AI capabilities also extends to service firms. Netflix stands out as a fascinating example of an organization pushing the boundaries of hyper-personalization. Individualized recommender systems analyze your history and behavior to suggest content you may enjoy. The story doesn't end there: the system also presents the content in a way that appeals to you. For example, if you're a thriller fan, the blurb for a series or movie emphasizes that aspect. If you prefer comedy, the humor element is highlighted in the blurb.

Taking analytics to the next level, Netflix also captures 'implicit signals': how long you watch a show, which parts you rewind or fast-forward. While these inputs are, of course, fed into the recommender system, the information is also used to refine programming. The casting of the lead character (Kevin Spacey) and much of the cast in *House of Cards* was driven by data analytics and pattern generation.[16,17]

Content curation for education, news updates, counseling, and a host of other applications is another obvious example. Learning effectiveness increases manifold when the delivered

---

16 'Netflix Harnesses Big Data To Profit From Your Tastes', Forbes, 21 June 2021, Netflix Harnesses Big Data To Profit From Your Tastes (forbes.com)

17 'How Big Data Helped Netflix Series House of Cards Become a Blockbuster?', SofyTV, How Big Data Helped Netflix Series House of Cards Become a Blockbuster? - Sofy.tv - Blog

content aligns with your preferences for media (text vs. audio vs. video), language (idiom used, etc.), and other parameters. For instance, the system scans your browsing and viewing history and concludes that you're a cricket fan. Leveraging this insight, it creates cricketing analogies to explain the basics of physics, thereby sparking your interest.

Customer pull

Having tasted the early benefits, customers are now demanding hyper-personalization, rewarding brands that deliver and penalizing those that do not. According to a 2021 global survey (one can reasonably expect figures to have increased since then), 71 per cent of consumers expect personalized interactions.[18] Companies that personalize experience 40 per cent higher revenues, while reducing customer acquisition costs by a whopping 50 per cent.[19]

The time has come

While Gen AI is the magic wand that brings hyper-personalization to life, it's worth mentioning that the concept of creating unique personal experiences was first expounded by C.K. Prahalad and M.S. Krishnan in their book, *The New Age of Innovation: Driving Cocreated Value Through Global*

---

18 'The value of getting personalization right—or wrong—is multiplying', McKinsey & Company, 12 November 2021, The value of getting personalization right—or wrong—is multiplying | McKinsey

19 'What is personalization?', McKinsey & Company, 30 May 2023, What is personalization? | McKinsey

Networks.[20] The idea, succinctly encapsulated in the formula N=1, stated that value creation should focus on the individual customer, and they must receive a 'unique, personal experience.' Pathbreaking work indeed, given that the book was published in 2008, well before the true ramifications of AI, let alone Gen AI, were understood.

BEHIND THE SCENES

Delivering a hyper-personalized customer journey is akin to developing a video game. Dozens of storytellers conceive a compelling plot. Thousands of permutations of potential gaming moves are mapped out and their effects fed into the system, enabling smooth progression of the storyline, regardless of whether the user has chosen to shoot or knife the enemy combatant. Hundreds of designers create top-tier, realistic graphics. Hundreds of technicians work behind the scenes to ensure the user experience is seamless and as perfect as possible. In short, the back-end is complicated, comprising myriad flawlessly interwoven components.

In a similar vein, the ramifications of hyper-personalization are expansive, reshaping the conventional framework of an organization.

1. Explosion in the number of SKUs

Catering to the specific needs of customers necessitates creating multiple variants of a product – known as Stock Keeping Units (SKUs) in business parlance. SKU #1: white

---

20 'The New Age of Innovation: Driving Cocreated Value Through Global Networks', C.K. Prahalad, M.S. Krishnan, McGraw-Hill Education, 2008

linen shirt with white buttons, SKU #2: white linen shirt with colourless buttons, SKU #3: white linen shirt with button-down collar, and so on. As personalisation increases, so do SKUs.

2. Extensive inventory management

A proliferation of SKUs implies increased complexity in managing inventory. Determining, managing, and optimising inventory levels and warehouse management for each SKU is a task best handled by AI, which first helps decide the right number of SKUs.

3. Flexible manufacturing

Swelling number of SKUs is a manufacturing nightmare. Shrinking batch sizes for conventionally mass-produced products spell disaster for financial returns.

Traditional manufacturing processes require retooling for each variant (depending on changes in specifications between SKUs), which negatively impacts cost and turnaround time. Flexible production systems, designed to adapt to product modifications and variations in order size, are the solution.

Additive manufacturing, or 3D printing, is a flexible technology that allows for a wide range of product modifications without retooling. Designs sent to the machine in the form of computer-aided design (CAD) or 3D models are printed instantly, providing agility in production or the option to pivot between products. 3D printers don't require tooling like traditional machines, allowing small quantities of each SKU to be printed ('manufactured', to borrow the nomenclature of a bygone era) without adding to the cost.

4. 'Edge manufacturing' or 'anywhere, anytime manufacturing'

With flexible manufacturing and the elimination of traditional tooling-based machinery, manufacturing can be undertaken from virtually anywhere. Local production, sized for the region, is rapidly becoming more cost-effective on the back of additive manufacturing.

Consider 'edge computing,' an architecture that enables computation closer to the user's location, reducing latency. Edge computing refers to running applications from centres near you rather than thousands of kilometres away, in say, Rio de Janeiro. This decentralised computing model mirrors decentralised manufacturing. Hyper-personalisation, akin to edge computing, is driving the rise of 'edge manufacturing.'

Versatility is a major asset. If winter arrives earlier than expected, instead of being stuck with season-inappropriate inventory, designs for winter wear can be transmitted instantly to additive manufacturing facilities, printed within minutes, and delivered to stores. In-store 3D printing (as high-end brands might do) cuts distribution costs.

However, decentralised manufacturing comes with a catch: distribution complexity. If additive manufacturing facilities aren't co-located with retail stores, transportation routes multiply requiring complex logistics optimisation. Yet, with Gen AI and other advanced technologies, this challenge is easily manageable.

Say goodbye to massive factories mass-producing products that need to be transported hundreds of kilometres to retail stores. The new manufacturing paradigm ushers in decentralised and on-demand production, sounding the death knell for the concept of economies of scale and mega factories. As Schumacher's famous book title goes, *'Small is Beautiful'*.[21]

5. Multitudinous communication packages

Customisation of a product or service, complemented by bespoke communication, exponentially boosts the likelihood of purchase and strengthens customer relationships.

Announcing the availability of a variant curated for a specific customer (or, in reality, a small group, though the recipient doesn't need to know that) requires reaching out with a tailored communication package. This package conveys not only the existence of the offering but also does so in a manner attuned to the recipient: message, tone, creative style, mode of transmission, and so on. As the number of variants increases, so too does the number of unique communication packages.

Over time, the sheer scale of diverse communication packages reaches a tipping point, beyond which it's impossible to humanly manage every variant without employing a large army of marketing specialists. Fortunately, technologies such as Gen AI can easily convert intent into reality. The only workable formula is to have one, or a manageable number, of core generic communication packages layered with Gen AI-driven customisation.

Nurturing customer relationships leads to enhanced sales in the long term. It builds loyalty, which is the elusive yet strongest competitive advantage for a brand. Gen AI

---

21 'Small Is Beautiful: a study of economics as if people mattered', Ernst Friedrich Schumacher, Blond & Briggs (1973 – 2010), HarperCollins (2010 – till date)

enables customisation packages that delight customers and foster stronger affiliations. For example, Zomato adopted a simple yet effective tactic on Father's Day. When purchasing through Zomato, customers could share their father's name to generate a personalised message, delivered by a celebrity. While the only 'customised' element of the message was the father's name, ensuring it was seamlessly integrated into the conversation is the real challenge. By using numerous voice samples of the speaker, AI generates the correct tone and intonation the celebrity would have used.

While the focus of this example is on driving sales and customer relationships, a similar approach applies to after-sales customer service.

6. Vendors, and more vendors

A consequence of the vast array of product variants is a potentially larger vendor base. Take the example of a sports shoe company: in addition to a vendor for shoe laces, the brand would need a supplier for Velcro (for those who don't want laces) and elastic materials (for customers who prefer slip-on shoes rather than fastening them with laces or Velcro).

Identifying, onboarding, and managing these new vendors adds to the operational challenges organizations will face. A significant proportion of these vendors will be marginal, forming a long tail of suppliers. 'Marginal' doesn't refer to the size of the vendor but rather to the procurement (how many adults would opt for LED running shoes?) and regional (how many adults around Kohima would prefer Velcro shoes?) perspectives.

7. Technology as the heart

Technology powers and nurtures hyper-personalisation. The resultant operational complexity requires near-complete reliance on Gen AI and complementary deep technologies, such as additive manufacturing and big data analytics.

Managing the sheer volume of variants in SKUs, communication packages, and logistics optimisation exercises is beyond human capacity. Identifying potential customers, forming relevant homogeneous segments, generating product concepts, demand forecasting, tracking, and monitoring products — from production to sales or excess inventory — is most effectively handled by Gen AI and similar technologies. Flexible manufacturing, the bedrock of enabling bespoke production, is underpinned by deep technologies.

The flip side of this heavy dependence on technology is the transition of human roles from 'doing' to 'overseeing'. The extraordinary combination of advanced algorithms, the ability to manipulate and analyse massive volumes of data, create content, and harness phenomenal computational power makes human intervention impractical. Our job now is to direct the Gen AI system to the appropriate information sources, clearly lay out the objectives of the exercise, highlight any red flags (such as racist social media posts), and, at best, perform a common-sense check on the output.

JUMP-STARTING YOUR COMPANY

From the customer lens, the allure of hyper-personalisation is irresistible, and straggling companies will struggle to retain their clientele. Read on for eight pointers to ensure your company doesn't miss the train.

1. Hyper-personalization: front and centre

Galvanise your company into adopting hyper-personalisation. Chances are your competitors have already embarked on the path, some more than others, particularly if you're in a business-to-consumer sector. An individualised offering is at the inflection point, swiftly transitioning from a customer delight add-on to a customer expectation. Falling behind spells doom.

2. Invest in technology

Technology is the steel frame supporting hyper-personalisation. Investing in access to a reliable, fit-for-purpose Gen AI system, supplemented with appropriate deep technologies, is core to business sustainability. Set aside a separate budget for Gen AI; the allocation hinges on your preferred execution option (buy vs. pay-per-use, or variants thereof). As mentioned earlier (Chapter 3), factor in expenses related to activities such as fine-tuning the model, regular updates, and periodic maintenance. Your technology team may also need to expand or adapt.

3. Strengthen processes and systems

High-quality historical data in sufficient volume is the fuel that powers the Gen AI engine. Acquired and generalized external data, or poor internal data quality, results in sub-optimal outcomes. Instituting robust systems and processes to capture and store data will ensure your company is positioned to leverage Gen AI effectively.

4. Ahoy, all on-board

Technology and data, combined, resemble an amusement park with no people. Employees breathe life into the hardware and software. Sensitise your staff—across hierarchy levels and functions—to the emerging paradigm. Excite them with the possibilities that hyper-personalisation offers. Introduce the team, particularly production, to the shift towards flexible manufacturing. Some roles may require additional training.

Change worries people, and the complexity of operations under Gen AI can be intimidating. Address these concerns early rather than letting them fester into resistance.

5. White elephant mega factories

The new manufacturing paradigm is upon us. Decentralisation of production, marking the end of mega factories, is a reality, not wishful thinking. While the pace of transition may differ between companies, late adopters are at risk of being left behind and facing extinction. Prudence dictates reassessing decisions related to establishing massive new manufacturing facilities. Otherwise, your company could be left with a white elephant as the production world evolves. Re-thinking centralised manufacturing is crucial.

6. Exporters, beware!

Exporters and export-oriented units will suffer the effects of localised production. As international brands increasingly opt for close-to-customer manufacturing, foreign suppliers will lose business. Consumer brands like luxury and high-street apparel, bags, and shoes are likely to be early adopters. Many of these companies currently outsource the bulk of their production to low-cost manufacturing destinations such as China, Bangladesh, Sri Lanka, Vietnam, and India.

Acknowledging the trend is the first step for affected businesses. Next, explore alternative strategies. Scouting for new customers is one option, although it's a temporary fix given the ubiquity of decentralised production. Following international brands by setting up local production facilities is another route. But adding value to the brand in ways that localised production cannot is a winning strategy, even if identifying and delivering the specific 'value-add' is challenging. Finally, many suppliers to international brands are large, sophisticated organizations themselves, and may consider pivoting their business models—transitioning from tier 1 suppliers to brands.

7. Recasting the team

The criticality of this aspect warrants special emphasis, despite being touched upon in earlier pointers and other megatrends. Adopting hyper-personalisation impacts the optimal staffing structure across departments—from marketing to data analytics to finance.

Arguably, the production function is the most severely impacted. Shifting from the traditional mega-factory model to decentralised and localised production triggers a large-scale geographic reallocation of employees. Moreover, additive manufacturing, much like automation, involves fewer people to operate and manage the process, with low-skilled labour bearing the brunt of the contraction. The handful of operators required to run the 3D printers also need to be technically qualified. Farewell to the conventional semi-literate worker.

Massive reskilling and retraining initiatives should be on the cards for organizations, alongside potential retrenchments.

8. Continuous innovation

Choosing to adopt hyper-personalisation is just the beginning. Deriving value—the crucial element of success—is contingent on discovering the right triggers for customising products or services. Innovation workshops are a useful tool to identify intervention nodes and prioritise them based on impact, feasibility, cost, and other parameters.

Keep in mind that this is not a one-time exercise. Establish a quarterly rhythm to fine-tune ongoing initiatives while ideating for new nodes. Finally, recognise the omnipresence of this programme across the organization. Accordingly, the core Innovation Team should include representatives from all functions (and not just marketing, as is typically the case). Ideas should be sought from all employees, especially from on-the-ground sales and production personnel.

JUMP-STARTING YOUR CAREER

Exciting as it is for consumers, hyper-personalisation could have a significant impact on your professional journey. Two pointers to mitigate any unpleasant surprises:

1. Assess your role

Evaluate the impact of hyper-personalisation on your role. Will it require more or different knowledge and skills? Will it be minimally affected in the short to medium term? Or, will it cease to exist? Will the role shift elsewhere?

2. Remould yourself

Inevitably, the Gen AI era will necessitate reinventing yourself across multiple dimensions. Two of the most obvious facets include:

- Relocation: As manufacturing and distribution become decentralised and move closer to customers, be prepared to relocate if you're involved in these disciplines.
- Upskill and reskill: As mentioned earlier, the production function is likely to be the hardest hit. Depending on your specialisation, reskilling may be necessary to function in the new world of Gen AI. For example, learning about additive manufacturing technologies would keep you relevant if you're in an engineering department. Additionally, reskilling can open up new opportunities for you—new roles that didn't exist before, such as 3D printing or behavioural sciences to better understand individual customers, among many others. This aspect is covered in greater detail in the trend *IQ: for whom the bells toll*.

CHAPTER 5

UNPREDICTABILITY AND IRRATIONALITY

THE SECRET INGREDIENTS OF COMPETITIVE STRATEGY

Generative AI took the stage,
Its wisdom the height of the age.
Yet, unpredictability,
Its true archenemy,
Kept its genius locked in a cage.

– ChatGPT, on being prompted to "create a limerick on generative artificial intelligence and unpredictability as Gen AI's nemesis"[1]

---

1 Created and retrieved on 5 August 2024

> *The battle between corporates, each leveraging Gen AI to drive their corporate strategy resulting in a status-quo, terminates only when a player makes an unpredictable or irrational move. Consequently, lateral thinking to generate creative, unconventional concepts becomes a competitive advantage.*

THE RATIONALE
BATTLE OF EQUALS

Survival itself is success in the corporate jungle. Despite the meticulously cultivated "we are good guys" image and reams of value statements purporting generosity of spirit, inter-organizational rivalry is intense and cut-throat. A company may have the best-in-class product, but if competition convinces the customer otherwise, the enterprise in question is ruined. The 'qwerty' keyboard layout is a case in point. Scientific evidence proves it is the worst of many options. However, the corporates invested in the 'qwerty' layout succeeded in persuading consumers to stay with the 1876 format.[2] No wonder, then, that competitive strategy—the art and science of gaining and sustaining an advantage over

---

2 'Why we use the QWERTY keyboard layout — and why it's probably not the best design', ZME Science, 30 April 2023, Why we use the QWERTY keyboard layout — and why it's probably not the best design (zmescience.com) ; 'QWERTY – Best or Worst Keyboard Layout', Geeks for Geeks, 29 April 2021, QWERTY - Best or Worst Keyboard Layout - GeeksforGeeks

competitors, or, as a corollary, preventing competitors from maintaining theirs—takes on paramount importance.[3]

Literature on the levers to out-compete rivals, termed 'competitive advantages', abounds. The classical advantages, proposed by the legendary Michael Porter,[4] pertain to cost and differentiation. Can you deliver your products or services cheaper than competition, while achieving parity or proximity in the bases of differentiation? Can you introduce unique attributes to your products or services which are valued by customers? A related nuance is focus—limiting the scope of your target segment(s). Your offerings cater to a specific section(s) of the market, from a cost or differentiation angle. Over time, academicians and strategists have suggested various builds or variants. One is predatory pricing—pricing lower than competitors regardless of cost, to rapidly build market share. Another is the network effect—where the value of a product, service, or platform rises exponentially as the number of users increases. For this book's purposes, given it is not a treatise on competitive advantage, suffice it to say that these multiple options only add to the complexity.

At its core, the basic questions that competitive strategy seeks to answer remain unchanged: Where should your company go? How should it get there? Four elements underpin a robust strategy:

---

[3] Definition of competitive strategy adapted from 'Competitive Strategy', Science Direct, 2003, Competitive Strategy - an overview | ScienceDirect Topics

[4] 'The Competitive Advantage: Creating and Sustaining Superior Performance', Michael Porter, 1985, The Free Press

1. Access to accurate and thorough data—on the market, existing and potential customers, financials, etc.
2. Competitor and ecosystem intelligence
3. Big data analytics to develop patterns and scenarios
4. Knowledge of corporate strategy as a discipline: theory, case studies, analogies (such as war tactics)

Since logic is the base fabric, AI is perfectly suited for these tasks. Where data is incomplete, Gen AI's prowess with probability and pattern generation becomes handy.

Designing competitive strategy is much like playing chess, Go, or Magic: The Gathering. Superficially, the objectives differ—capture the opponent's king, control territory, or overpower with spells and creatures—but in all three, the key to winning is developing forward scenarios and optimizing each move. Smarter systems mine historical responses to prioritize likely scenarios. And yes, the system pivots as often as needed—without, unlike human strategists, a flicker of frustration.

If your company had access to a relentless ace strategist of that calibre, wouldn't you use it fully? Unfortunately, so would your rivals.

Now consider a situation where strategy teams across competitors also use Gen AI to guide actions. Think of two Deep Blue systems—or equally matched AI engines—playing chess. Both understand every rule, have access to every tactic, and the capability to compute millions of scenarios. The outcome? Almost certainly, a stalemate.

Introducing an anomaly is the only way to break the stalemate. Fans of *The Matrix* series will recognise the parallel:

the Integral Anomaly is exempt from following the rules of the system, enabling him[5] to alter the game. In the business world, an anomaly can stem from an unexpected (or irrational, in computer parlance) action, proprietary information, or a novel new factor. Either—or a combination of these—can instigate a disruption of the status quo. None are mutually exclusive, nor subject to rigid definition boundaries.

In hindsight, everything is obvious. What seems like an irrational action today can, years—or even months—later, be interpreted as a logical reaction to an unmet consumer need. Or proprietary information might be seen as having revealed a white space no one else recognised at the time. Admittedly, the difference between 'irrational' and 'proprietary information' is tenuous, lying in the extent of analysis undertaken at the idea inception stage. For clarity, visualise a graph, with probability of success on the x-axis and depth of analysis at the ideation stage on the y-axis. 'Irrational', the first approach, lies in the low probability of success and negligible analysis quadrant. 'Proprietary information', on the other hand, sits in the high-high quadrant. Of course, 'high' on either axis is a misnomer—it's a relative term. In reality, what's considered 'high' here would be 'unacceptably low' in any conventional analysis.

This chapter focuses on the first approach—unpredictability or irrationality as a super-weapon to win the battle. (The other two approaches are explored in the following chapters.) An anomaly can be introduced either through human

---

[5] Trivia for those who may have hazy memories of The Matrix trilogy: The One or Neo is considered the Integral Anomaly

intervention or via a deliberate hallucination of the Gen AI system. Hallucination is AI lingo for false or inaccurate information churned out by the system.

THEORICAL AT BEST?

Is the entire notion of injecting unexpectedness or a spanner-in-the-works merely a theoretical construct? Are there examples of absurd ideas that turned into winning bets? Yes—many more than one might assume.

On the absurdity scale, **Pet Rock**, would probably be off-the-charts. Gary Dahl, an advertising executive and freelance copywriter in California, decided to convert a jocular idea sparked off over drinks, into reality.[6] Launched in 1975, *Pet Rock* was a plain, everyday rock, packaged in a cardboard box with ventilation holes and straw bedding. A tongue-in-cheek manual on how to care for your rock was included. It went viral—and the craze transformed Dahl into an overnight millionaire.

A further, though less outrageous, evolution of this is virtual pets. *Tamagotchi*, a Japanese brand, lets you watch the birth of and raise an alien egg on Earth.[7] Somewhere between

---

6 "The Unbelievable Story of The Pet Rock: How One Man's Idea Made Him Millions!", Medium, 5 April 2023, "The Unbelievable Story of The Pet Rock: How One Man's Idea Made Him Millions!" | by Chris Jones | Medium ; 'The History Of The Notorious Pet Rock', Groovy History, 5 December 2017, Groovy History

7 "I raised a virtual pet', Deccan Herald, 22 July 2023, 'I raised a virtual pet' (deccanherald.com) ; 'Retro-Game Rides Nostalgia Wave As Tamagotchi Goes Back To The Future', Forbes, 12 June

an animated video and a basic game, it lives in a keychain-sized device. The 'owner' must feed it, clean it, play with it, discipline it, and manage a host of other activities. Launched in 1996, *Tamagotchi* became a craze in Japan and the US in the 1990s and 2000s. As of 2023, it had sold over 91 million units, spawning several other virtual pet platforms.

Behavioural science experts might argue that the human desire to nurture—combined with loneliness—is a well-known trait. Add fast-paced lifestyles, limited space, and financial constraints (the monthly cost of maintaining a Great Dane is around INR 18,000–20,000, according to some estimates), and the success of non-physical pets becomes obvious. In retrospect, the reasoning is irrefutable—but at the time of ideation, virtual pets—let alone pet rocks—were considered outlandish.

The yellow smiley face is now a global icon—a yellow circle with black oval eyes and a black arc for a smile. Legend has it that Harvey Ball, a Massachusetts-based artist, created it in ten minutes, responding to a request from State Mutual Life Assurance Company for a morale-boosting design.[8] No blue-blood corporate strategist or next-gen AI system would have bet on its business potential. It's the kind of doodle a teacher draws on a school assignment.

But Franklin Loufrani, a journalist in France, thought differently. In 1971, eight years after Ball's smiley debuted

---

2023, Retro-Game Rides Nostalgia Wave As Tamagotchi Goes Back To The Future (forbes.com)

[8] 'The $500m smiley face business', The Hustle, 24 March 2023, The $500m smiley face business - The Hustle

in US culture, Loufrani trademarked it and distributed ten million free smiley stickers. The rest is history. Mars (chocolates), Levi's (jeans), Agfa (film), and many others licensed the smiley. Today, Apple and Microsoft use it, too. The Smiley Company now earns an estimated USD 500 million annually through licensing deals.

Historians and psychologists can only explain it in hindsight. The US and much of Western Europe—especially France and Germany—were still recovering from the turbulence of the 1960s: Vietnam, anti-establishment protests, and social unrest. The smiley symbolised the "feel good" emotion people were longing for.

The tech world has its own share of wacky ideas that shattered the valuation ceiling.

In October 2007, two unemployed art school graduates, starved for funds to pay the rent of their three-bedroom apartment in San Francisco, hit upon an idea that could only come from extreme desperation: rent out mattresses for an overnight stay in their apartment to attendees of an upcoming design conference.[9] They hoped someone would take them up on the offer, given the overcrowded hotels and skyrocketing room rates. Thus was born Airbnb!

It was a difficult start for Brian Chesky and Joe Gebbia (later joined by Nathan Blecharczyk)—a tale that should have

---

9 'The Inside Story Behind the Unlikely Rise of Airbnb', Knowledge at Wharton, 26 April 2017, The Inside Story Behind the Unlikely Rise of Airbnb - Knowledge at Wharton (upenn. edu) ; 'The Airbnb Story by Leigh Gallagher', book extract, Leigh Gallagher, February 207, Penguin ; 'The Airbnbs', Paul Graham, December 2020, The Airbnbs (paulgraham.com)

ended before it started. Friends and investors alike assured the founders that Airbnb was a terrible idea. The standard refrains were: "You guys are crazy." "There's going to be a murder in one of these houses. There's going to be blood on your hands." "I am not touching this with a 10-foot pole." Brian Chesky recounts an investor walking out midway during the meeting. They assumed he was going to the bathroom. As it happens, he didn't return. "He didn't even finish his smoothie!"

Another story comes from Snapchat. The utility of a mobile app where shared photos disappear within seconds was unclear.[10] The founders, Evan Spiegel and Bobby Murphy (also Reggie Brown, who later bowed out), went on to reject a USD 3 billion offer from Facebook and created a USD 27 billion company.[11]

While these examples represent vastly different sectors, the common thread is the wackiness or irrationality of the concept at the time of inception. Rigorous analysis, extensive data manipulation, or meticulous market research could neither have envisioned these ideas nor predicted their success. Lateral thinking led to the birth of these unique concepts, not the most sophisticated Gen AI systems. Only a niggling sixth sense, combined with human bravado, could have brought them to life. The outcome: companies with a powerful strategic edge. Leveraging out-of-the-box

---

10 'Snapchat Founders Prove That Turning Down Facebook's $3 Billion Wasn't Such a Bad Idea After All', 17 November 2016, New York Magazine, Snapchat Founders Prove Turning Down $3B Was Pretty Smart (nymag.com)

11 Approximate market capitalization, as of 28 June 2024, SNAP Stock Price | Snap Inc. Stock Quote (U.S.: NYSE) | MarketWatch

thinking is equally applicable for sparking innovation within a department or function, thus boosting the organization's competitive advantage.

JUMP-STARTING YOUR COMPANY

Illustrations make for fascinating stories to recount in public. But, is there a structure to induce quirky ideas? Ironic as this question sounds, the answer is yes. Below are five pointers to equip your company to transition into the next orbit.

1. Recruit dark horses or Anomaly Architects

Ideas, especially trailblazing and unorthodox ones, are the silver bullets of the future. Originality requires an off-beat and unconventional mind. Some people are naturally creative, but 'natural' is a misnomer—creativity is shaped largely by a person's upbringing and exposure. Diverse experiences spur imagination, like the ability to draw analogies from different fields and adapt solutions to a new context. For example, distilled learnings from customer service in a call center could be refashioned for the chemicals sector.

Anomaly Architects are not traditional management professionals—the ones who enter a specialized path (say, marketing or human resources) and stay on the narrow course. Classical candidate profiles such as "ten years of marketing in the consumer durables sector for a white goods company" are now obsolete. Organizations need to look outside the box for recruiting dark horses. Flexibility in experience and qualifications, coupled with a willingness to take a chance on off-beat applicants, is imperative (more on risk appetite below).

2. Spawn lateral thinking

Complement the recruited pool of Anomaly Architects by building a tribe of lateral thinkers from within the existing employee base. Brilliant, innovative ideas can come from anyone, often the most unexpected person. Energize the workforce through exposure to creative thinking techniques.

3. Overhaul to integrate

Creating a cohort of Anomaly Architects, whether through recruitment or cultivating creative thinkers internally, is just the first step. Deriving value from their presence requires introducing supportive processes and systems as well as integrating Anomaly Architects into the organization.

Co-existence of roles that rely on lateral thinking, alongside those that are procedure-oriented, in the same organization necessitates a comprehensive overhaul of systems in line with the skillsets, deliverables, and outcomes required in the Gen AI era. Performance appraisal principles and promotion criteria are among the frameworks demanding recast. Unpredictable action, the new competitive superpower, thrives on unconventional thinking. At the same time, certain functions will (rightly!) be subject to concrete KPIs or require strict process adherence.

A fall-out of the diverse roles and the cohabitation of multiple structures within an organization is internal cultural tension. Creative mavericks and archetypical strait-jacketed professionals can coexist, but demands serious effort. Their mindsets and work styles are typically vastly different. Ensuring mutual respect—understanding and appreciating the value each brings to the organization—is the magic formula. Both parties must feel that the organizational systems reward them fairly.

4. Enjoy bungee jumping

Wielding the unpredictability super-weapon requires a willingness to play with fire. Risk tolerance and risk capacity are the two foundational pillars. Creating a risk-tolerant environment entails providing a psychologically safe space for employees to express their ideas, paired with systems that facilitate execution. Risk capacity refers to the financial resources an organization can allocate to bear failures.

A risk-tolerant or high-risk appetite organization is characterized by unorthodox processes that encourage and support taking chances—like granting executives the power to make gut-based decisions on seemingly illogical grounds. This privilege should extend across domains: from strategy to recruitment (refer to the point on inducting dark horses into the team).

Organizational culture and systems aside, risk-taking is an expensive proposition. Stringent but innovative financial management boosts a company's risk capacity. Simple actions, such as carving out a specific budget for moonshots and staying within that pool of funds, help lower investor perception of the company's riskiness, thus reinforcing confidence.

5. Redefine failure

Failure is par for the course; after all, an overwhelming majority of Bohemian ideas, by definition, will fail, or they wouldn't be Bohemian. In the traditional worldview, failed initiatives are frowned upon and penalized—an attitude that stifles maverick ideation. New-age mindsets and systems must encourage taking the plunge into unchartered realms by rewarding the generation and piloting of such ideas. Maintaining the status quo, for most roles, should actually be 'frowned upon and penalized.' Put differently, review your definition of failure.

6. Take your ecosystem along

Bygone is the era of the lone wolf competing with other lone wolves. "A company does not compete, its ecosystems compete," succinctly summarizes one of the principles of competing in the digital age, as laid out by Dr. Ram Charan in his book *Rethinking Competitive Advantage*.[12] The increasing complexity of each element in the value chain forces the outsourcing of many to specialists. Delivering a high-quality customer experience—whether for a product or service—requires that all parts of the system synergize, sparing no effort.

Take the Nokia versus Apple battle, which started in 2006[13]. By then, Nokia was an established market leader in mobile phones, selling around half a billion devices annually, supported by a tightly controlled supply chain and strong relationships with key telephony service carriers.

Meanwhile, companies like Google were preparing for the impending smartphone era, recognizing that traditional bases

---

12 'Rethinking Competitive Advantage: New Rules for the Digital Age', Ram Charan, April 2021, Currency

13 'Apple's Rise and Nokia's Fall Highlight Platform Strategy Essentials', Forbes, 9 March 2013, Apple's Rise and Nokia's Fall Highlight Platform Strategy Essentials (forbes.com)

of competition—quality products at competitive pricing, brand reputation, and distribution—were being upended by a new factor: availability of applications (apps). Games, communication tools, information apps, and utilitarian apps—the broader the selection, the more appealing the phone brand. Building an app library is an entirely different ball game, prompting giants like Google to partner with individual developers and small software firms. Even billion-dollar entities were forced to eat humble pie, persuading 'tiny' developers to create apps for their platforms.

Ironically, Nokia was invited by Google to join the Open Handset Alliance, a multi-company group aimed at building an open-source operating system for smartphones. Nokia refused. Soon after, Apple launched its app store, attracting tens of thousands of developers. In fairness, Nokia did attempt to build an app store, Horizon, but six months after its launch, it had only 60 apps. A key reason for this failure was Nokia's inability to effectively engage with the ecosystem, particularly the developers. The impact on Nokia was severe and swift— its market capitalization plummeted from GBP 110 billion in 2007 to GBP 14.8 billion in 2012.

Recently, the smartphone ecosystem has expanded to gadgets and services such as smartwatches, tablets, and smart home devices.[14] While companies like Apple and Samsung have thrived, Nokia is still struggling.

---

14 'Why Nokia Is Not Competing with Mega Brands Like Apple and Samsung', Global Technology Review, 21 June 2024, Why Nokia Is Not Competing with Mega Brands Like Apple and Samsung (globaltechnologyreview.com)

JUMP-STARTING YOUR CAREER

Expect Gen AI to displace many mainstream roles across functions. New-age professionals such as Anomaly Architects and innovators will be in demand. Here are some actions you can take to build your relevance and ensure you're in a sustainable job category.

1. Raise your Gen AI Quotient

Gaining a basic understanding of the implications of Gen AI, a recurring theme across trends, is essential for your survival. Focus specifically on the impact it will have on your area of specialization.

2. Boost your Creativity Quotient (CQ)

Does the Eureka moment, the radical out-of-the-box idea, appear out of nowhere, or is it a matter of training? Is creativity a gift reserved for a select few, or can it be learned? While the jury is still out on this debate, here are some tips for raising your Creativity Quotient (CQ).

   a. The scientifically-minded have developed numerous frameworks to facilitate wide-angle exploration of ideas or pathways to attain objectives. Mastering these models expands your repertoire of potential solutions, enhancing your CQ.

   b. Study historical examples of innovative strategies to draw inspiration for your specific context. One impactful example is Amul, which revolutionized India's dairy industry. Rejecting the traditional system of middlemen, the Gujarat Cooperative Milk Marketing Federation

(GCMMF) formed a cooperative owned by farmers. This gave farmers independence and fair, consistent payment for their produce. Additionally, Amul eschewed celebrity advertising in favor of the Amul Butter Girl, a beloved character since 1966.

c. Reading about diverse disciplines provides fodder to transpose ideas. For instance, linking military strategies with music theory might help you devise a winning plan for your production-related challenge. More on this in the trend *IQ: For Whom the Bells Toll*.

d. Participating in diverse activities (like contemporary dance or jazz music) or joining groups (such as book clubs) broadens your horizons. Having friends from varied backgrounds and professions expands your perspective even further.

e. Finally, playing strategy-oriented board games such as Chess, Go, and Risk sharpens your ability to map out possibilities.

CHAPTER 6
THE TREASURE HUNT FOR TRIVIA

Generative AI, quite the whiz,
Crafts stories and poems with a fizz.
But with cultures so varied,
It sometimes gets harried,
And nuances may go amiss.

– ChatGPT, on being prompted to "create a limerick on generative artificial intelligence and cultural nuances"[1]

---

1   Created and retrieved on 5 August 2024

> *In a world of perfect information and data analytics, proprietary information provides a competitive advantage. Gleaning cultural and behavioural nuances of mini communities constituting the target market is an exemplar of such non-public information. This marks the dawn of behavourial scientists and Culture Explorers in the corporate arena.*

THE RATIONALE
CHANGING FACE OF TRUE TREASURE

Flashback: up to two decades ago, knowledge—or information—was the true treasure, the manna for winning against competition. Were you aware that a new expressway was being constructed between two of your key markets, enabling rapid re-deployment of products in case of a demand-supply mismatch in one location? Or did you catch the news that a new policy affecting your industry was being rolled out?

The rise of the internet, followed by the explosion of big data repositories around the turn of the century, triggered the age of information democratization. What you know no longer matters as much—because everyone has access to the same information. What you do with that data—how you manipulate it—makes the difference. Enter: data analytics as the competitive edge. Population and demographic statistics are freely available to all, but it's the slicing, dicing, and analyzing of those figures to derive actionable insights that determined an organization's success.

Determined, not *determines*—because the reign of data analytics is rapidly coming to an end, as GenAI takes centre stage. Access to vast amounts of data, layered with machine-generated algorithms and code, trained to detect patterns, signals the quietus of not just quantitative data-based insights but also implied qualitative analytics as a lever of competitive advantage. Mining mobile phone data from millions of customers to determine hourly usage peaks and troughs (quantitative analytics), or monitoring social media posts to ascertain reactions—known as sentiment analysis (qualitative analytics)—is now most accurately and rapidly undertaken by AI. As such applications become commonplace, the resulting analysis or outputs are no longer differentiators and offer little competitive edge.

With the strategic value of conventional levers fast dissipating, new sources of competitive advantage are emerging in an otherwise perfectly balanced AI vs AI landscape. One such panacea is proprietary information—either insights only you are privy to, or a unique perspective on publicly available data.

Cultural and behavioural nuances gleaned only through lived experience—and not statistical data—about, say, Goan Catholic Kshatriyas (called *Chardo* in Konkani) is an example of non-public information. These imperceptible aspects of life can only be discerned through immersion in the community or through extensive interaction with Chardos. "Community" or "tribe," in this context, can range from location-based (such as South Mumbai), to origin or identity-linked (such as

Parsis), to mixed or intentionally formed (such as metro-city, affluent, Indian classical music lovers). On-ground nuggets are the real pot of gold at the end of the rainbow.

Another way to uncover proprietary information is to view a situation through a different lens. It's common knowledge that giant dog breeds like St. Bernards, Mastiffs, and Great Danes drool heavily, making cleanup a constant chore for their owners. Pet parents would naturally appreciate an easier solution. A variation is to observe human behaviour or preferences closely—to detect lifestyle patterns that others have either overlooked or dismissed as irrelevant.

The elixir lies in converting such proprietary insights into meaningful customer offerings. Hence, the hunt for proprietary information—or trivia.

PROPRIETARY INFORMATION IN PRACTISE

The **Sony Walkman** is an iconic example of leveraging behavioural and cultural nuances to transform the arena. Origin stories vary, as is often the case with legends. During his frequent beach trips with his children, Akio Morita, the founder of Sony, was often subjected to loud music from old-fashioned boomboxes.[2] Nothing could be done about teenagers and their music craze, so everyone bore the nuisance, which lasted from morning till the wee hours. Morita decided

---

2 'The history of the Sony Walkman', Ural Federal University blog, The history of the Sony Walkman (urfu.ru) ; 'The Walkman', Time magazine, 1 July 2009, The Walkman | TIME ; 'Case Study: a global phenomenon born out of frustration', Clustre blog, Case Study: a global phenomenon born out of frustration | Clustre, The Innovation Brokers

to change the status quo and instructed his engineers to build a portable music player which, importantly, could be attached to a person's head. This way, music buffs could quite literally carry their music with them—while cycling, walking, travelling on the metro, or sitting by the beach—without disturbing anyone around.

Another version credits Masaru Ibuka, Sony's co-founder and honorary Chairman, who once remarked to his team, "I wish it was easy to listen to recorded music on the airplane," especially on long flights. The result: the first Walkman, designed by engineers eager to please the Chairman. Akio Morita, then CEO, decided to commercialise the product without conducting market research. "The market research is in my head; we create markets," he is believed to have stated. Those familiar with the Japanese approach to business will recognise that skipping market research was a bold—and conventionally unacceptable—leap of faith.

Regardless of which version of the tale you prefer, the Walkman was launched in Japan in 1979. Sony expected to sell about 5,000 units a month, but over 50,000 were sold in the first two months alone. Word spread like wildfire, and children in the US and Europe began asking for the product even before its planned international launch.

Closer home, a similar tale of deep customer understanding led to a transformative innovation: **sachets**. The story begins in Cuddalore, a port town in Tamil Nadu, south of Chennai. Originally called Koodalur—meaning 'confluence' in Tamil—the town sits at the intersection of three rivers: Penniyar, Gedilam, and Paravanar, and has been ruled by various empires, from the Pallavas and Vijayanagar to the Marathas, Tipu Sultan, and later the French and English.[3]

Chinni Krishnan, a local farmer-turned-entrepreneur dabbling in pharmaceuticals and FMCG, sparked India's sachet revolution, triggering a profound social change. He was disturbed by the sight of unkempt children and adults, the cause being obvious: lack of affordability.[4] Personal hygiene products such as talcum powder and Epsom salts were sold in minimum 100-gram tins or glass bottles, placing them out of reach for low-income communities (factory and farm workers, for instance). Unlike the monthly buying patterns of middle-class consumers, the relatively disadvantaged purchased items for daily or weekly use, in sync with their income cycle.

"Whatever I make, I want the coolies and the rickshaw pullers to use. I want to make my products affordable to them," Krishnan would say. In the 1970s, he hit upon a novel solution: repackaging talcum powder in 20-gram packs and

---

3   'Cuddalore District', Government of Tamil Nadu, About District | Cuddalore District, Government of Tamilnadu | Sugar bowl of Tamil Nadu | India ; 'Cuddalore District', Tamil Nadu toursim, Cuddalore | Tamil Nadu Tourism (tn.gov.in)

4   'The man behind the sachet revolution in India', Madras Musings, January 1 – 15, 2021, The man behind the sachet revolution in India Madras Musings | We Care for Madras that is Chennai; 'CavinKare – Shampoo sachet that was the true pioneer of Middle India market', The Print, 12 November 2022, CavinKare – Shampoo sachet that was the true pioneer of Middle India market (theprint.in) ; 'All You Need To Know About The 'Sachet Revolution' In India In Early 80s', Marketing Mind, 29 May 2021, All You Need To Know About The 'Sachet Revolution' In India In Early 80s - Marketing Mind

Epsom salt in five-gram sachets. He soon realised that liquids too could be packaged in sachets, and expanded the idea to include hair oil, honey, and shampoo.

The sachet revolution, however, wasn't as simple as dividing a large tin into smaller pouches. Packaging innovation was key. Krishnan's initial attempt to modify a PVC sealing machine to secure a transparent hose pipe failed. After many experiments with different materials, he finally arrived at a workable solution.

Following Krishnan's untimely demise, his sons discovered their family house was mortgaged, and the bank was threatening to auction the property unless the loan was repaid immediately. Building on their father's idea, the elder son, Dr Rajkumar, launched the Velvette brand of shampoo, sold in sachets for Rs 2. Its tremendous success led the younger son, C.K. Ranganathan, to establish CavinKare.

Soon, other FMCG brands—who had previously ignored rural and low-income markets—jumped on the bandwagon.

Yet another example from a vastly different sphere is the **Austin Seven**, or the **Morris Mini-Minor**. Love it or hate it, you can't mistake its distinctive appearance for any other car.

The Suez Canal crisis of 1956 spurred the creation of these vehicles. Egypt, under President Jamal Abdel Nasser, nationalized the Suez Canal on July 26, 1956; it had previously been managed by Compagnie Universelle du Canal Maritime de Suez, a French-British colonial-era company.[5] As a result,

---

5 'The Suez Crisis, 1956', Office of the Historian, Department of State, USA, Milestones in the History of U.S. Foreign Relations - Office of the Historian (state.gov)

petrol flipped from being a cheap, abundant commodity to an expensive and rationed one in the UK. Sales of large, fuel-guzzling cars plummeted, giving way to low-fuel-consuming German bubble cars (aptly named for their appearance, which resembled a covered scooter or rickshaw—depending on your aesthetic).

Leonard Percy Lord, the head of the British Motor Corporation (BMC) at the time, reportedly hated the bubble cars so much that he vowed to rid the UK's streets of them.[6] He tasked his ace engineer, Alec Issigonis, with designing a "proper miniature car"—a small, affordable, fuel-efficient vehicle capable of ferrying four adults. Specifically, the car should fit within a 10×4×4-foot box, with 6 feet of the 10-foot length reserved for passengers. To save costs, it should use an existing engine unit.

So convinced was Leonard Lord—or perhaps driven by his single-minded desire to eliminate the bubble cars—that no

---

6 'The September 2023 Auction, Lot 153', Manor Park Classics, Lot 153 - 1959 Morris Mini Minor De-Luxe (manorparkclassics.com) ; 'Collectible Classic: 1959-2000 BMC Mini', Automobile magazine, October 2009, 1959-2000 BMC Mini - Classic Mini Cooper - Automobile Magazine (archive.org) ; 'Obituary, Jack Daniels', The Guardian, 15 December 2004, Jack Daniels | Automotive industry | The Guardian ; 'Mini - a brief global history of the world's most loved car', BMW group website, MINI - A BRIEF GLOBAL HISTORY OF THE WORLD'S MOST LOVED CAR (bmwgroup.com) ; 'Research vs Vision: the origin story of Sony Walkman, Mini Cooper, and the iPhone', Medium, 22 September 2022, Research vs Vision: the origin story of Sony Walkman, Mini Cooper, and the iPhone | by Taras Savytskyi | UX Collective (uxdesign.cc)

market analysis or research was conducted. Lived experience pointed to the urgent need for a low-cost, highly fuel-efficient small car.

Alec Issigonis' pioneering design embodied the adage: "The harder the struggle, the more glorious the triumph."[7]. As instructed, he used an existing engine: BMC's 848 cc in-line four-cylinder unit. The ultra-compact engine-transmission configuration featured a transversely mounted engine mated with a specially developed transmission to ensure a shared lubrication system. To save space, Issigonis opted for front-wheel drive, which allowed 80 per cent of the car's floor to be used for passengers and luggage. Traditional coil springs were replaced with small rubber cones built into the car's subframe.

After a preview for the press in April 1959, the Mini was officially launched in August of that year. Initially, its radically different appearance was met with resistance. However, test drives quickly won over potential customers, and within a year, the car was a huge success for BMC. The Mini remains an iconic fashion statement in the 21st century, thanks to its legacy, which continues under the BMW Group.

JUMP-STARTING YOUR COMPANY

Transforming intent into action is complex, especially when the interventions are not as clear-cut as "construct another plant in location X." Below are four pointers to help formulate an execution plan for your company.

---

7 Quote commonly attributed to Sivananda Saraswati, a yoga teacher and spiritual guru (1887 – 1963)

1. Lay out the red carpet for behavioural scientists

Uncovering cultural or social norms is the central to acquiring proprietary information. Contrary to popular belief, discovering unique and useful insights requires specialized knowledge, expertise, and skills that traditional corporate managers lack. Anyone may experience a singular Eureka moment, but staying competitive in the Gen AI epoch demands continuous flow of proprietary information, calling for a formalized and systematic ideation engine.

Enter: behavioural scientists, a discipline including sociologists, anthropologists, psychologists, and related fields. Strictly speaking, social sciences study human society, while behavioural sciences focus on actions. Colloquially, however, "behavioural science" is often used as an umbrella term. Behavioural scientists, trained to track social patterns, are the tribe that will distil proprietary information.

2. The dawn of Culture Explorers

On-ground customer intelligence does not emerge from desk research. If sifting through encyclopaedias were the magic formula, given today's immense and democratized data mining capabilities, the result wouldn't be proprietary information!

Localized revelations emanate from people who live within the target community. A tribe of perceptive and inherently empathetic individuals, keen to learn about other cultures—the Culture Explorers. This cohort would be a valuable source of insights about existing and potential customers, which could lead to modifications in the offering or marketing communication, or even ideas for new offerings.

An argument could be made that the deepest and sharpest nuances about a community would stem from an indigenous member. While this is undoubtedly true, perceptive local talent who understands your organization's imperatives may not always be available. Replicating this on-the-ground intelligence playbook across different segments is crucial for maintaining an edge over competitors, underscoring the need for Culture Explorers as a new class of employees.

3. Prep your organization

Behavioural scientists and cultural explorers are radically new entrants into the corporate arena, bringing fresh perspectives and different ways of working.

The flip side is the discomfort amongst industry veterans, many of whom are unused to professional interactions with such groups. To derive value from this change in expertise, extra effort will be needed to ensure these cohorts gain organization-wide acceptance and integrate with existing employees. Similarly, legacy processes and systems designed for traditional corporate functions will need to be altered.

4. Leap of faith

"Some people say, 'Give the customers what they want.' But that's not my approach. Our job is to figure out what they're going to want before they do. People don't know what they want until you show it to them. That's why I never rely on market research. Our task is to read things that are not yet on the page."[8] — Steve Jobs, founder of Apple.

---

8   Steve Jobs interview, BusinessWeek, 25 May, 1998. Web link unavailable.

Jobs was echoing Henry Ford's famous statement from nearly a century earlier: "If I'd asked customers what they wanted, they would have told me, 'A faster horse!'"[9]

Corporate historians are skeptical whether Henry Ford actually said this, but the sentiment resulted in the birth of the Ford Motor Company and its legendary Model T car. Ford's disregard for customer preferences also echoes his other famed statement, "Any customer can have a car painted any colour that he wants so long as it is black," made during a 1909 sales meeting.[10]

Customer insights are foundational, but how you act on them determines your success. Robust managerial practices dictate scientific analysis and scrupulous hypothesis testing. Many iconic products, though, didn't emerge from asking customers their needs or conducting elaborate market research surveys. Sachets, the Morris Mini-Minor, or the Sony Walkman entered our daily lives without pre-launch analytical proof of their success. They were based on intuition or sharp observation of human behaviour followed by, quite literally, a leap of faith.

---

9   'Henry Ford, Innovation, and That "Faster Horse" Quote', Harvard Business Review, 29 August 2011, Henry Ford, Innovation, and That "Faster Horse" Quote (hbr.org)

10 The quote appears in Henry Ford's co-written autobiography, "My Life and Work," published in 1922, although historians have not found an independent verified newspaper story that recorded the comment. 'True or False: Did Ford really say "Any color the customer wants, as long as it's black"?', Collectors auto supply website, 3 November 2021, True or False: Did Ford really say "Any color the customer wants, as long as it's black"? - Collectors Auto Supply

Creating an organizational framework that supports leaps of faith involves multiple interventions, from granting executives no-questions-asked decision powers, to accepting failures, to adjustments in performance evaluation criteria. This is similar to the "enjoy bungee jumping" concept discussed in the earlier chapter.

JUMP-STARTING YOUR CAREER

Mentioned below are three pointers to ensure you benefit in the era of Cultural Explorers.

1. Carpe diem (Latin for 'seize the day')

The Gen AI paradigm ushers in new domains into the corporate arena, offering you a chance to reinvent yourself—either by shifting to a different area of specialization or expanding the scope of your responsibilities. Consider it an opportunity for mid-career self-discovery. Do the behavioural sciences interest you? A combination of, say, marketing expertise and an understanding of human behavior or social interactions is an unparalleled asset for the company and would position you uniquely in the organization. Becoming a Cultural Explorer is another option.

2. Amplify your Cultural Quotient

Whether or not you choose to be a Cultural Explorer, discerning and leveraging the lifestyle nuances of communities is a pivotal talent in the emerging era. Employ one or a combination of the tactics below to boost your cultural quotient:

a. Cultural quotient, a concept introduced over two decades ago by Professors P. Christopher Earley and Soon

Ang,[11] is gaining popularity in the corporate sphere, particularly from a Diversity, Equity, and Inclusion (DE&I) angle. Many learnings and techniques, though, are transferable. Encourage your company to organize courses on enhancing cultural intelligence and make the effort to participate in these training programs.

b. Self-study is another route to building your cultural quotient. Read about different societies, focusing on existing and potential customer communities. A sensible starting point might be "tribes" closely allied with yours—provided they are your target market.

c. Actively seek or create opportunities to interact with people from diverse backgrounds to widen your exposure to the plethora of sub-cultures around us. Some of the insights you gain may provide valuable behavioural insights for your organization.

3. Remove blinkers

The new paradigm "blows with the winds of change"[12] in the composition of corporate employees, shifting from a largely homogeneous team to a mosaic of specializations, personalities, attitudes, and working styles. Learning to appreciate and integrate the resulting diversity in perspectives boosts the quality of decisions and, therefore, your success in a Gen AI-enabled organization. Contrary to popular belief,

---

11 'Cultural Intelligence', P. Christopher Earley and Soon Ang, Stanford University Press, 2003

12 Quoted from 'Wind of Change', a song by Scorpions, released on 21 January 1991

accepting the unfamiliar is tougher than expected. Time ossifies our way of thinking, doing, and acting. Professional interactions with colleagues from traditionally non-business disciplines may feel new (and, possibly, uncomfortable) for many. Gear up by keeping an open mind, ready to absorb diverse viewpoints.

CHAPTER 7

EXPERIENCE
THE GREAT COMEBACK

Generative AI, with its might,
Crafts wonders both day and night.
Yet the personal touch,
That we cherish so much,
Is a gift only humans get right.

– ChatGPT, on being prompted to "create a limerick on generative artificial intelligence and personal human touch"[1]

---

1   Created and retrieved on 5 August 2024

> *Forging personal relationships with the company's immediate ecosystem is a powerful mode of supplementing Gen AI's superior analytical and pattern creation abilities. Accordingly, organizations should harness the external networks of experienced employees, shifting from a transactional Point of Contact model to a relationship-led Personal Ally approach*

THE RATIONALE
BACK TO THE PAST

Digital technology heralded the season of the young. Contemporary education curricula, which include exposure at an early age, cemented the generation's position as masters of technology. Old-world managerial practices are seen as exactly that—'old world'. A fresh set of crown jewels emerged in the business world: the energy of youth, technology savviness, quantitative over qualitative, and rigid processes trumping the human touch. Experienced top management and professionals were relegated to the back rows, if at all they had a place in the new theatre. The new mantra: CEO at age 30, retired (or a variant of that) by late 30s.

Gen AI turns these new beliefs on their head. As the Terry Jacks chart-topping smash hit goes, "…we had seasons in the sun… But the hills that we climbed were just seasons out of time."[2] Technology is no longer the toy of the young for several reasons.

---

2 'Seasons in the Sun' is the English-language adaptation of the 1961 Belgian song "Le Moribond" ("The Dying Man") by singer-

Gen AI signals a new epoch of user interface. One that is intuitive and easy-to-use, accessible even to the visually challenged through applications such as text-to-voice converters. Knowledge and ability to use, therefore, are no longer a deterrent, dissolving the young generation's dominance over technology as an ace.

The analytical speed of the management team is conventionally seen as an asset. Gen AI combines data processing capabilities with self-learning and creation, ensuring the accuracy and pace of analysis far exceed human ability. At the same time, the system can recommend appropriate decisions for routine operational matters, with the scenario complexity it can handle increasing rapidly. The ask from humans is no longer endless hours of grunt work (think: verifying financial records, ensuring compliance with regulations, highlighting discrepancies, etc.); instead, unconventional thinking or action is paramount.

In the Gen AI versus Gen AI corporate battle—a fast-emerging reality where competing organizations leverage Gen AI with equal dexterity—the search for the elusive anomaly to break the tie is the solution. Two modes of thwarting the balance were discussed in the earlier chapters. Introducing an additional factor, one that is beyond the (current) capability of technology, into the equation is the third approach.

Unsurprisingly, the maverick element stems from what defines us as quintessentially human: interpersonal relationships and trust. Gen AI can create 'smart' systems

---

songwriter Jacques Brel. The song was a worldwide hit, in 1974, for Terry Jacks and, later in 1999, topped the charts in the UK for Westlife

but lacks the ability to understand the intricacies of human bonding. Trust, in business, as in any context, is not built overnight. It takes decades of association, of assisting each other in small ways, often unrelated to work. Helping your supplier's daughter get into college, advising the distributor on a suitable mobile model for her grandfather, and such like. In many ways, this is a throwback to the past when personal touch and relationships mattered. You did business with people you knew and trusted.

This calls for experienced hands, people who have been in the business for years, who know vendors not as vendors, but as unique individuals with whom they've shared many laughs. Moreover, as argued in the previous chapter, *The Treasure Hunt for Trivia*, decoding cultural nuances unlocks success in a Gen AI-driven business strategy. Often, a keen understanding of preferences and behavioral undertones rests with the gray-haired. Consequently, older professionals will command greater prominence and relevance in the organizational structure, reversing the current trend of replacing all old-timers with young blood. The clamour for young top management will also temper (and already has, particularly in non-core technology sectors), with fit-for-purpose, not age, being the criterion. This is a trend culminating from the confluence of Gen AI and the increasing productive lifespan of adults due to better healthcare.

DOES IT REALLY MATTER?

Relationships sound lovely, but do they actually deliver any concrete benefits? A valid concern, most compellingly answered through real-world examples.

Hugely underrated, yet critical, is the personal relationship between a salesperson and distributor. Trust and an implicit favour-for-favour mutualism often enable the end-of-year 'transfer of goods' from company to distributor, ensuring that the company meets its sales target. Distributors also serve as rich sources of competitor intelligence and can strongly influence customer or retail distributor purchases. A similar analogy applies across the value chain, such as with third-party SME manufacturers.

Another example of the pivotal role of personal relationships and trust is one most will resonate with—servicing or repairing your air-conditioners, fridge, car, and the like. Most of us are clueless about the mechanics of these machines and rely on trusted technicians to resolve issues. Whether it's transmission failure, worn brake pads, or a faulty alternator, a visit to your reliable car garage—and typically, a specific person in the outfit—is the solution. Inevitably, the choice of garage or engineer isn't determined by qualifications (which, in any case, aren't always available!), but primarily by trust.

Paradoxically, as the world rapidly embraces automation, Gen AI, and other deep technologies, the value of the personal touch—the trusted confidante—amplifies exponentially. At the end of the day, people still prefer to speak with other people, not machines, regardless of how sophisticated or human-like they may be. The healthcare and education sectors provide clear examples of this behaviour.

The craze to consult specialist and super-specialist doctors for every minor or non-serious ailment is waning. Patients increasingly recognize the comfort and irreplaceable value of seeking advice from their decades-old general practitioner, someone who knows their and their family's medical history. In contrast, specialists often come and go—a gastroenterologist today, a dermatologist tomorrow—lacking the personal touch or enduring relationship.

In the world of education, many observers predicted the end of physical schools. The early days of the pandemic demonstrated that online teaching was feasible, cheaper, and could be delivered from the comfort of home. However, by the end of the pandemic, online fatigue set in, and both teachers and students were eager to return to physical classrooms. Teaching requires more than just technical delivery—it needs human-to-human interaction, extending beyond the set agenda of each session.

JUMP-STARTING YOUR COMPANY

Attitudinal shifts are some of the hardest to implement in organizations. Below are three pointers to assist your company's transformation.

1. End of PoC. Emergence of PA.

Traditional organizations appoint Points of Contact (PoC) to interact with each of their ecosystem entities. At least, the more structured ones do. Others often struggle, leading to confusion and lack of accountability internally ("who is responsible for ensuring the packing material arrives on time? That's not my job") and externally ("who should I approach for payment? I keep getting passed around").

Robust management practices dictate mapping all third-party entities the company engages with, from technology providers to distributors to financiers and suppliers. A specific person or team, called the Point of Contact (PoC), is typically appointed as the liaison between the external organization and your company, usually a process-oriented manager or team tasked with negotiation, tracking deliverables, and follow-ups. These tasks can now largely be handled by advanced Gen AI systems.

In the Gen AI era, replace the PoC with a Personal Ally (PA)—an individual or team entrusted with the responsibilities of the PoC, while also developing and strengthening relationships with ecosystem players. Leveraging Gen AI for routine or operational tasks frees up valuable time for the PA to focus on the human aspects of the relationship.

Depending on the nature of the business and the size of its external network, instituting PAs across the board could be an onerous task. In such cases, prioritize partnerships. A common oversight is restricting the focus to suppliers and distributors; instead, scan the value chain for critical third parties. Identifying relevant employees who have deep bonds with decision-makers in prioritized external entities is the next step. When assigning PAs, be mindful that having a partner's contact coordinates or having interacted with them is not the same as a personal relationship.

Human connection takes time to nurture; it is not an overnight process. Sometimes, the strongest bond may lie with a former employee, who may need to be brought back, full-time or on a contract. Build a pipeline of PAs for each key third party to ensure a smooth transition when the time is right. The Private Banking sector, with its focus on personalized service (despite the lack of effectiveness in many banks), offers a parallel. The more astute banks have shifted from a one-to-one Relationship Manager model to a team model, ensuring continuity in case of retrenchment.

2. Redesign people systems

Effective roll-out of the Personal Ally (PA) program requires revamping the existing human resources framework. While not a new concept, no concrete reward is attached to relationship building and management. Introducing PAs in this scenario yields minimal value from an otherwise powerful and future-resilient strategy. In fact, 'minimal value' can quickly turn into a burden on the organization, with the perception being that an army of PAs is engaging in an activity not seen as reward-worthy by the company.

Redesigning the system starts with recruitment. For the right candidates, the ability to build relationships, including a track record of doing so, should be a mandatory criterion. A common misconception is equating extroversion with success as a PA. Remember, the objective is forging a personal connection, not identifying the life-of-the-party! Finally, don't overlook the existing employee base – some of the best candidates may already be part of your company.

Retaining the PA cohort in a competitive talent market is the next challenge. The ability to build a personal bond requires empathy and other intangibles, which cannot be acquired in a flash. Unlike, say, distribution optimization algorithms, which can be learned in months, the prerequisites for being a PA are developed over years due to social conditioning and upbringing. High-impact PAs will be in short supply, making it essential to have a strong internal structure to support and reward them. Employee performance assessment systems for PAs must include relationship building and strengthening as key elements. The criteria must reflect the three realities of human interactions: they take time to develop; benefits land in bursts (immensely useful information or assistance after years of simmering); and the best efforts don't guarantee a strong personal bond.

3. Energize the organization

Systems are futile unless humans drive them. Even the best frameworks fail without employee support. Sensitize all employees, whether they interact externally or not, on the new Gen AI paradigm, particularly the value of human touch as a competitive advantage.

Be prepared for resistance, especially from traditional thinkers who may not see the relevance of softer aspects in the workplace. Time-consuming as this task may be, getting employees on board will ensure success. Other groups that should be mobilized include Board Members and shareholders.

JUMP-STARTING YOUR CAREER

Paradigm shifts requiring a mindset change are an opportunity for you to shine. While a few of the pointers below, at a macro 100,000-foot level, may seem similar to those mentioned in the earlier trend, the specifics differ.

1. Ride the tide

'There is a tide in the affairs of men ... Which, taken at the flood, leads on to fortune'[3]. Seize the opportunity that Gen

---

3 'Julius Caser', Shakespeare, 1599 - 1600

AI is presenting to you. Do you have the interest and mindset to be a Personal Ally (PA)? While the role can be learned, the passion to pursue it is key to success. The role of the PA is still being fully fleshed out, offering you the chance to shape your responsibilities, instead of having a human resources specialist dictate terms. Moreover, from an organizational perspective, you would be seen as an extremely valuable and future-proof employee.

2. Boost your Emotional Quotient (EQ)

Forging human connections is likely the toughest and trickiest skill, requiring both art and science. Age-old studies into what makes some people more prone to developing relationships continue. While hypotheses abound, the cold fact is that scientific study is still far from identifying verifiable answers.

In the meantime, experts have developed techniques and approaches to help accelerate your journey toward forming successful relationships. Heightening your emotional intelligence is a proven aid. Emotional intelligence, or emotional quotient, consists of four dimensions: self-management, self-awareness, social awareness (including the ability to empathize with others), and managing relationships or social skills. The latter two pillars are especially relevant for adding a human touch to interactions and building personal connections. Regardless of whether you're a Personal Ally, developing your EQ is worth the investment. Fortunately, numerous courses are available to help with this.

3. Butress your position

Act now. Start developing or strengthening your bond with the external ecosystem, even if your organization hasn't formally implemented the Personal Ally system yet. Whether you're part of the technology team, marketing, finance, or any other team, chances are you interact with a third party. Demonstrating your relationship-nurturing capability positions you firmly as a prized employee and PA candidate, mitigating any risk of retrenchment as Gen AI becomes more integrated into the company.

CHAPTER 8

THE CLINICALLY EMPATHETIC ORGANIZATION

There once was an AI so keen,
With empathy built in its sheen,
It could learn and create,
But when asked to relate,
It proved that machines can be seen.

– ChatGPT, on being prompted to "create a limerick on generative artificial intelligence and empathy"[1]

---

1 Created and retrieved on 13 August 2024

> *Gen AI is propelling organizations up the empathy ladder, through culturally sensitive, individualized communication and raising red flags to the people team when an employee is fatigued, over-worked or the like. However, it is common knowledge that this empathy is system generated, not the result of a caring colleague – 'clinical empathy', perfect in all respects yet lacking authenticity and soul.*

THE RATIONALE
... AND THE WORLD WILL LIVE AS ONE[2]

Until the mid-twentieth century, teachers had a free hand to enforce discipline and adherence to rules, such as caning or a rap on the knuckles. Today, in more progressive schools, similar practices are antiquated and, thankfully, prohibited – an educational approach steadily trickling down to the next tier of schools.

The evolution of corporate culture mirrors this. Yelling at colleagues or voicing racist remarks are relics of the past. While Europe leads the charge in eliminating unacceptable behavior, other societies, including some Asian companies, are slowly but surely following suit. Hamlet's dilemma of 'to be, or not to be: that is the question' is now redundant; this a transformation that is already in motion. For starters, the foot soldiers of present-day corporate world, millennials and

---

2 'Imagine', John Lenon, released 1971

Gen Z,[3] unlike earlier generations, vocally push back and are unforgiving of autocratic management styles. This heightened sensitivity aligns with the growing demand for organizations to embrace diversity, equity, and inclusion (DE&I). People-sensitive, diverse, equitable, and inclusive defines the organization of a fast-approaching tomorrow.

Technology is traditionally viewed as the antithesis of humanness – cold and impersonal. Gen AI inverts that notion, enabling personalization at a level that humans struggle to achieve. Your past behavior provides the structure for building your persona. The system mines social media, company databases, and other sources to create messaging that resonates with you, amplifying chances of a positive response. Applied across the organization, Gen AI creates a profile for all employees, helping, for instance, Employee X draft an email to Employee Y with a high likelihood of achieving the desired outcome.

Gen AI drafts emails, memos, etc., for review. Refining the language based on the recipient's personality profile further enhances effectiveness. For example, concise, task-oriented language for some, and a friendlier tone for others.

Gen AI also incorporates cultural nuances into communication. 'Culture' refers not just to community culture (geographic or racial) but also corporate culture (for example, FMCG company X is less formal than FMCG company Y). Addressing the former class of culture is tricky. Avoiding

---

3   Millennials and Gen Z are those born circa 1965 to 1980, and 1981 to 1996 respectively

stereotypes and prioritizing personality over clichés is an effective way to overcome this bias.

The system will even recommend the most effective form of communication—text, voice, or in-person—tailored to the message and recipient. This approach can be extended to strategic external stakeholders: vendors, distributors, customers, financiers, and technology providers.

EVERY MOVE YOU MAKE

The next level integrates images and videos captured by office CCTV, echoing the unsettling lyrics of the hit song 'every breath you take, and every move you make ... every step you take, I'll be watching you.'[4]

Subtle physical gestures—eye twitches, blood rushing to the cheeks, slight changes in voice pitch—provide real-time cues about an employee's current state of mind, allowing messaging to be fine-tuned. Linking wearables such as personal activity trackers provides data on heart rate, blood pressure, and more, enabling greater individualization of communication. Basic analysis could highlight fatigue or loss of concentration, triggering actions like time off or raising red flags for overworked staff. Collecting this data raises privacy concerns, which, while pressing, are not discussed here.

HUMAN VERSUS AI

The obvious question is whether humans surpass Gen AI in creating bespoke communication. Perhaps in a one-off case, under certain circumstances. However, humans lack

---

4 'Every Breath You Take', The Police, 1983

the consistency and range, especially when both are needed. Switching from your natural style of communication to another requires effort and training. You might pull it off occasionally, but doing so repeatedly is difficult. Additionally, the ability to attune to a different personality is colored by your mental state at that particular moment. Moreover, few personas may be so diametrically opposite to your own, that 'walking the footsteps of a stranger'[5] may not be possible. Gen AI, on the other hand, can tirelessly replicate millions of personality types on a consistent basis, completely oblivious to its own irritation, bad days, or similar emotional vicissitudes. Game, set, match: Gen AI.

IMPLICATIONS

Messaging and actions tailored to each employee's preferences and traits will reshape the very fabric of an organization and its people. Two of the most profound impacts are the rise in expectations and the increase in cynicism.

Rising bar

Heightened sensitivity to personal circumstances and cultural context defines the current corporate zeitgeist. Gen AI's ability to enable greater individualization of messaging will only push up the expectation bar. Rude or culturally insensitive emails, or any other form of communication, will be inexcusable. Feigning ignorance about a team member burning out will appear disingenuous. The red line on acceptable behavior at

---

5 'Colours of the Wind', Judy Kuhn (from the movie Pocahontas), 1995

work is tightening. Welcome to the era of the empathetic organization – culturally aware, designing experiences based on your personality and mindful of your moods.

Missing: the soul

Paradoxically, the rising expectations fuel greater cynicism.

It's common knowledge that Gen AI formulates communication and triggers actions like sending birthday cakes or flowers at just the right time. This often signals the end of the warmth or joy you feel towards a colleague who reached out to you. Spot a paragraph in an email checking in on your health after sick leave or inquiring about your exciting holiday at the end of a trip to Goa, and the widely held belief is that this is a Gen AI-generated message, not genuine concern from a colleague.

Niceties, in the times ahead, will be viewed with cynicism, based on the assumption (and rightly so in most cases) that they're Gen AI-generated. R.I.P., authenticity; human emotions and traits will be addressed with clinical precision.

At its current stage of evolution, Gen AI can simulate 'sensitive' output constructed from gigabytes of data and pattern generation, but it does not understand human emotions. This is like reproducing Picasso's cubist artwork with geometric precision – the result is flawless, though devoid of character and soul. Much like Gen AI-generated communication.

The only counter to this is taking the time and effort to personalize messages by adding your unique human touch.

JUMP-STARTING YOUR COMPANY

At first glance, the shift to a more empathetic organization may seem dictated purely by technology. Purchase and install the appropriate software – mission accomplished. But this is far from the reality. A structured transition requires several elements to align. Jump-start your company's journey with the following pointers.

1. Form the Empathy Team. Garner the arsenal

Gen AI, unlike humans, is not intuitive. Technology doesn't individualize messaging based on a 'sense' of the person. Instead, it analyzes extensive historical information such as formal personality assessments and past emails of the employee to form patterns, which are then used to create bespoke communication.

As a first step, form an Empathy Team to identify the necessary relevant information. This isn't a squad of Gen AI experts. While technologists are part of the mix, the team leans heavily towards human behavior and communication specialists. Psychologists, sociologists, and others who decode human nature play the leading role, not AI domain experts. Depending on your company's size and available in-house capabilities, bringing in external specialists may be necessary.

Groundwork done, it's time to roll up your sleeves. While most companies retain detailed financial records for decades, other inputs required for customization is not as readily available. The lead time for data extraction and collation can be lengthy, so it's best to start now. Simultaneously, implement processes for automated and seamless data collection going forward.

2. Balancing discipline

In the quest to become more sensitive, don't lose sight of the bulls-eye – the deliverables or outputs from each activity. A specific team member might be tired, another might not be in the mood to work, and yet another may want a day off. However, work still needs to be done. Striking a balance between empathy and discipline, between high-quality timely output and sensitivity, is critical for the organization to prosper. Clear disciplinary boundaries must be established, or your company risks sub-standard output.

3. Choose judiciously

Scrutinize off-the-shelf Gen AI products with built-in cultural sensitivity modules for contextual applicability. The relevant social and cultural milieu for the product may differ from your company's environment. For instance, the corporate culture in the USA is distinct from that of Japan, while Indian society contrasts starkly with German norms. Cross-hierarchy interactions in a tech company may be more casual than in a cement company. A tech-heavy top management speaks a different language from one dominated by MBAs, shaping the tone for the broader organizational culture.

Fine-tuning the off-the-shelf product is an optimal solution, unless, of course, your company can afford to build a bespoke system. Either way, global corporations must be mindful that each of their offices worldwide sports a unique ethos. The overarching company-specific ambiance forms the foundation, layered with local norms, making the vibe in the Cape Town office slightly different from that in the Singapore office.

The obvious question is: how much fine-tuning should be done? Should the system be further refined to account for variations between the Delhi and Mumbai centres? What about the headquarters in Mumbai's Nariman Point versus the sales office in Goregaon? Geography is not the sole criterion. A similar debate arises for personality types: what's the optimal number of permutations? There is no scientifically rigorous answer. Ultimately, it's a decision for top management, based on factors like available funds and the degree of cultural dissimilarities between offices.

4. Prepare the organization

Undertake a sober assessment of your company's position on the empathy scale. Bridging a large gap between the current and intended levels in a short period can be mentally unsettling for employees.

That said, taking baby steps isn't an option. Industry-wide standards and available Gen AI products set the minimum acceptable target rating on the empathy scale, not your company's current level. In this era of globalization, expect the floor rating to be high. Moreover, assume a literally overnight transition once the system is tested and goes live. Your company will leap from zero to one; there are no intermediate steps.

Another factor to consider is the pace at which the deadline for change is approaching. Many office workers already use Gen AI for drafting written communication, either for professional or personal purposes. In other words, the full-fledged progression to Gen AI-created messaging is well underway.

Prepare your employees for the rapid pace and extent of change by conducting diversity management workshops to help alleviate feelings of being overwhelmed.

JUMP-STARTING YOUR CAREER

It may be tempting to sit this trend out and take on the role of a silent participant. After all, the actions primarily fall under the organization's responsibility, not the individual employee's. Don't do that!

1. Get a head-start

The signs are clear: the empathetic organization is near, driven by Gen AI. Equip yourself by boosting your cultural sensitivity and emotional intelligence.

2. Understand your team

While tactics for enhancing your cultural quotient were discussed earlier in *The Treasure Hunt for Trivia*, what's particularly relevant to this mega-trend is mapping your team's cultural background. Identifying key contextual threads will help foster deeper connections and add a personalized touch to make your interactions with colleagues more authentic.

3. Feed into the design

Provide inputs on the boundaries for empathy in the workplace, ensuring that the balance between high-quality output and sensitivity is maintained. This is especially important if you lead a team and are responsible for deliverables. Responsibility without authority is a recipe for failure.

CHAPTER 9

TRUST
THE HALLMARK OF A WINNER

Generative AI's quite the feat,
But deepfakes can lead to deceit.
With trust as the shield,
True power's revealed—
A key advantage that can't be beat!

– ChatGPT, on being prompted to "create a limerick on generative artificial intelligence, the dangers of deep fake and emergence of trust as a competitive advantage"[1]

---

1   Created and retrieved on 19 September 2024

> *Trust is the newly minted source of competitive advantage propelled by the rise of deep fake and the criticality of personal relationships. Increased awareness of the manipulative potential of doctored media has heighted mistrust between an organization and its ecosystem. At the same time, in the AI versus AI battle for superiority between rival firms, personal relationships emerge as the trump card. Ultimately, in this duplicitous era of deep fakes, people prefer to do business with people they trust, making integrity a cornerstone for success.*

THE RATIONALE
DEEP FAKE: THE NEW DEMON
Is your mother real?

Post-lunch at 2:00 pm, your mother briefly video calls, urging you to try MyAachar's mango pickle. She swears it tastes just like nani's homemade raw mango pickle. Later in the day, your fashionista friend leaves a voice message urging you to check out G&L's newly launched trouser collection – formal yet trendy, just the way you like it. A few days later, when you meet your mother and friend in person, you discover, to your horror, that neither of them was on the video call. The voice, the visuals, and even their turn of phrase were indistinguishable from the 'real' thing. Science fiction? Not at all – this is today's grim reality. Welcome, deep fake!

The term originated in 2017 when an anonymous Reddit moderator using the pseudonym 'deep fake' introduced a subreddit where users posted videos swapping celebrity faces into existing pornographic videos. Today, 'deep fake' refers to any AI-modified media (text, images, video, or audio) that depicts real or imaginary people in fabricated settings. For clarity, the scene could be real – your office boardroom, for example – but the events and people in the scene are fabricated (hence, 'fabricated setting'). Synthetic media, a related and broader concept, refers to any media that is either generated or altered by AI. The key distinction is that while deep fakes are created with the intent to deceive, synthetic media encompasses both manipulations made for malicious or benign purposes.

Old wine in a new bottle?

Fakes, in themselves, are as old as history. Adulterated gold jewelry passed off as pure 22-carat pieces. Counterfeit luxury handbags from Louis Vuitton, Gucci, and Prada. Watches and electronics crafted in identical designs to Omega and Rolex, but at a fraction of the cost. The list goes on.

What sets deep fakes apart is their extraordinary level of sophistication and the limited ability of existing tools to detect them. Voice skins or clones, for instance, mimic voices with remarkable accuracy, down to the unique intonations. As a result, identifying false audio becomes a highly complex task.[2]

Generative Adversarial Network (GAN), a technique commonly used to create deep fakes, renders output that is

---

[2] 'What are deepfakes – and how can you spot them?', The Guardian, 13 January 2020, What are deepfakes – and how can you spot them? | Internet | The Guardian ; 'What is deepfake technology?', Tech Target website, What is Deepfake Technology? | Definition from TechTarget

imperceptible from the original. Essentially, GAN pits two AI engines against each other (designated as 'generator' and 'discriminator'). Assume the intent is to place you in Maitri, India's permanent research facility in East Antarctica. AI engine #1, the generator, cobbles together an image from a latent representation (a simplified version) or random noise. At this stage, the creation may look nothing like the end result. The second AI system, the discriminator, steps in to determine whether the desired output has been achieved and provides feedback to the generator. Back to the drawing board for the generator: based on the critique received, the generator churns out a revised version. The iterative process continues until the discriminator detects no flaws. Continuous learning covers any cracks in the armour. Think of Djokovic and Nadal engaged in a perpetual game of identifying and rectifying each other's weaknesses. A 2018 study by US researchers pointed out that people in deep fake videos don't blink. Once the paper was published, this Achilles' heel was swiftly amended.

While identifying deep fakes is a complicated process, creating one is relatively simple. Multiple applications exist. For instance, FakeApp, a desktop software released in 2018, allowed users with minimal technical expertise to easily swap faces in a video and share the altered output. Mobile apps, such as Reface and Zao, were launched as early as 2018-2019.

Unleashing the malevolent spirits of hell?

Deep fakes can, and indeed have, wreaked havoc with grave consequences across various fields. Besides entertainment, the political space is a prime target. A 2022 video depicted an ashen-faced Volodymyr Zelenskyy, President of Ukraine, directing his troops to surrender to the Russians.[3] A 2018 video showed Barack Obama, former President of the USA, calling then-President Donald Trump "a total and complete dipshit."[4] More recently, in the run-up to the 2024 US election, a political consultant for a rival candidate cloned President Joe Biden's voice using AI.[5] The resulting deep fake robocall urged voters in New Hampshire to refrain from participating in the Democratic presidential primary. Recognizing the severity of the situation, the Federal Communications Commission proposed a USD 6 million fine.

The corporate arena is not immune to deep fakes, with equally alarming consequences. In a 2019 video, Facebook founder Mark Zuckerberg was portrayed bragging about having "total control of billions of people's stolen data."[6] A

---

3 'Deepfake footage purports to show Ukrainian president capitulating', Reuters, 17 March 2022, Deepfake footage purports to show Ukrainian president capitulating | Reuters

4 'A video that appeared to show Obama calling Trump a "dipsh-t" is a warning about a disturbing new trend called 'deepfakes'', Business Insider, 18 April 2018, A video that appeared to show Obama calling Trump a "dipsh-t" is a warning about a disturbing new trend called 'deepfakes' | Business Insider India

5 'Democratic operative admits to commissioning fake Biden robocall that used AI', NBC News, 26 February 2024, Democratic operative admits to commissioning fake Biden robocall that used AI (nbcnews.com) ; 'A political consultant faces charges and fines for Biden deepfake robocalls', NPR, 23 May 2024, Criminal charges and FCC fines issued for deepfake Biden robocalls: NPR

6 'There's a fake video showing Mark Zuckerberg saying he's in control of 'billions of people's stolen data,' as Facebook grapples with doctored videos that spread misinformation', Business

statement of this nature could result in imprisonment for theft or, at the very least, massive fines and stringent oversight of the company. In 2019, the head of a UK subsidiary of a German energy firm transferred around GBP 200,000 into a Hungarian bank account following a call by a scammer mimicking the German CEO's voice.[7] Over the last few years, the stakes have skyrocketed. Early in 2024, a finance employee (using Alex as an alias) from a multinational corporation in Hong Kong paid USD 25 million to fraudsters impersonating the company's chief financial officer (CFO) over a video call. In fact, in addition to the CFO, Alex's other colleagues had also 'joined' the virtual meeting. Their presence heightened the authenticity of the interaction, giving Alex no cause to suspect foul play. As it turned out, all the attendees on the call were deep fake avatars.[8]

THE APPLE FROM THE GARDEN OF EDEN
Can you resist temptation?

Deep fake holds the potential to tarnish an organization's reputation, pose a security risk, and enable a highly sophisticated scam with enormous direct financial impact.

Insider, 12 July 2019, There's a fake video showing Mark Zuckerberg saying he's in control of 'billions of people's stolen data,' as Facebook grapples with doctored videos that spread misinformation | Business Insider India

7. 'What are deepfakes – and how can you spot them?', The Guardian, 13 January 2020, What are deepfakes – and how can you spot them? | Internet | The Guardian

8. 'What is deepfake technology?', Tech Target website, What is Deepfake Technology? | Definition from TechTarget

Fraudulent intentions aside, the primary desired outcome of deep fake is to influence behavior. The target is not merely existing and potential customers but the entire ecosystem—from vendors to distributors, from technology providers to financiers, even regulatory bodies. It aims to seduce potential customers into buying your brand, entice them to use the product more extensively, and drive frequent purchases. It also strives to persuade your value chain to choose you over competitors and bewitch policymakers to your side.

Indulging in outright deep fakes is a red flag for many respected or aspiring organizations. For one, the practice does not align with many organizations' values. Moreover, one can expect the introduction of laws to regulate the use of deep fake advertising or messaging by corporates.

However, deep fake is a spectrum along two dimensions: the degree of malicious intent and the extent of doctoring of the output. Easy availability of simple-to-use technology is likely to tempt organizations to employ a relatively less malignant version of deep fake. A phrase amended here, an expression altered there, an image edited elsewhere, voice re-modulated—small modifications, no scams, but still powerful impact. Touching up your photograph using common (and often free) applications such as Photoshop could be considered a rudimentary precursor to deep fake.

Driven by the game-changing payoff potential, the allure of deep fake may be too strong for some organizations to resist. While some may succumb to creating deep fakes internally, the 'smarter ones' will exploit unofficial channels. The uncontrollable nature of the web and social media, along with pervasive user-generated content, offers organizations a convenient buffer. An ostensibly unaffiliated person can be hired to create deep fake content that benefits the company, providing plausible deniability—commonly used by covert organizations or operations. If an issue arises, the organization can distance itself from the wrongdoers or, at the very least, deny any knowledge of their actions. Enthusiasts of international politics will recall the highly public Iran-Contra affair during the Ronald Reagan era—a classic example of 'plausible deniability'. Profits from weapons sales to Iran were allegedly funneled to the Contras, a counter-revolutionary group fighting against the leftist Sandinista government in Nicaragua. The dealings eventually came to light, and John Poindexter, former U.S. national security adviser, testified to Congress, "I made a deliberate decision not to ask the President, so that I could insulate him from the decision and provide some future deniability for the President if it ever leaked out." Could such a high-stakes strategy have been executed without President Reagan's knowledge? There is no definitive evidence either way.

Moreover, many offenders operate in niche social media circles, making it harder for regulators to identify such acts.

The beginning of the end of 'Trust'?

Trust becomes the casualty.

Historically, and even today, recipients of promotional material were skeptical, but there was a baseline trust. If a brand claimed a cooking time of five minutes, consumers braced for modest exaggeration, perhaps ten minutes, but definitely not an hour. Similarly, brands touting nutritional benefits were expected to inflate their impact, but consumers still trusted that some health perks would be delivered.

Deep fakes, however, take hyperbole and falsehoods to a completely new level—a fact consumers are now acutely conscious of. Growing awareness of the Machiavellian power of deep fakes is prompting audiences to view advertisements or messages with suspicion. The fear of being manipulated is eroding trust between organizations and their audiences, rapidly and severely.

Solidarité Sida, a French charity, created a deep fake video of then-President Donald Trump claiming "AIDS is over," ahead of a meeting of the Global Fund to Fight AIDS, Tuberculosis, and Malaria. While the intent may have been pure, the public was left distinctly uncomfortable.[9] A few other deep fakes have been well-received by viewers, but their impact on brand credibility remains unclear. Volkswagen used a 'retro deep fake' to promote its Golf GTI. Gene Kelly is shown dancing and singing in *Singin' in the Rain* alongside the Golf GTI, suggesting that, like the iconic movie, the car too survives reinvention.[10]

Further, the (correct!) assumption that deep fakes are often ahead of detection technology amplifies the general mistrust.

---

9 'French charity publishes deepfake of Trump saying 'AIDS is over", Euro News, October 2019, French charity publishes deepfake of Trump saying 'AIDS is over' | Euronews

10 'That's me singin' in the rain', BBC News, March 2005, BBC NEWS | UK | Magazine | That's me singin' in the rain

Even genuine messages are likely to be met with skepticism by a public aware that technological safeguards are insufficient.

In this climate of suspicion, any transgression—whether intentional, duped, or inadvertent—will be attributed to the organization. While culpability is clear in cases of intentional deep fakes produced by an organization, whether through official or unofficial channels, the other two situations are unfortunate.

Violations by someone the organization has genuinely not engaged with will be perceived as instigated by the organization. Typically, this could involve an independent social media influencer. Given the gravity of deep fakes, the probability of an innocent mistake by the errant individual is minimal. A larger conspiracy is almost certainly at play to malign the organization's reputation—a 'duped' transgression. This echoes a familiar military or political tactic, the 'false flag,' designed to appear as though it was perpetrated by a rival.[11] A notable instance is when Nazi operatives, disguised as Polish soldiers, attacked a German outpost in Gleiwitz, Poland, in 1939. Hitler used the incident to justify the invasion of Poland. More recently, Russian operatives disguised as local separatists to justify Russia's annexation of Crimea.

Inadvertent transgressions are more frequent than anticipated. Hallucination, where Gen AI fabricates answers or information when it cannot access authentic sources, results

---

11 'False flag', Britannica, False flag | Meaning, Operations, & Facts | Britannica ; 'False flags: What are they and when have they been used?', BBC, February 2022, False flags: What are they and when have they been used? (bbc.com)

in inaccurate information about the company or product. Clearly, the blame for this does not lie with the company, unless it knowingly released unauthentic information. However, from the victim's perspective, the organization is inevitably seen as the culprit.

TRUST: THE NEW COMPETITIVE ADVANTAGE
Much ado about nothing?

Yes, deep fakes are altering the trust equation between an organization and its stakeholders. Why ruffle your feathers? Is it all bark and no bite?

'Trust' features prominently in the values statement of nearly every organization, across sectors, geographies, and company sizes. From a practical standpoint, for most organizations, 'trust' and its offshoots like 'integrity' are often seen as the fluffiest of philosophies. Ethics committees purport virtues as a driver of business. Outside of these committee meetings, very few—including members of the hallowed council—truly believe that.

Gen AI rebuts this notion. As discussed in earlier trends, in the AI vs. AI battle for market superiority, personal relationships are the trump card. When tangible criteria are largely equal, people choose to do business with those they trust; consumers buy products from companies that have earned their trust. In this duplicitous era of deep fakes, trust is indeed a much-sought-after and uncommon attribute, which heavily tilts the balance.

Trust is the new competitive advantage. A core element in maintaining your company's edge over rivals.

The tentacles of trust extend far beyond deep fakes. Integrity in business dealings is a fundamental constituent. Since Gen AI is the nucleus of this book, traditional business ethics components are not fleshed out. Yet, in the age of AI, ethics and trust have become more important than ever. Do you honor contracts and agreements? Do you adhere to commitments to pay by a mutually agreed date? Do you transparently present accurate information?

Bear in mind the delicate yet potent nature of trust. Most traditional sources of competitive advantage, if lost, can usually be regained. For instance, if your product, marketed as a nutritious snack, is found to contain high quantities of trans fats, saturated fats, and added sugar, the product development team can work quickly to reformulate it to be rich in fiber, protein, healthy fats, and vitamins. Voila: the unhealthy snack turns healthy. Trust, on the other hand, once lost, is exceedingly difficult to regain.

Memory of elephants?

In earlier times, organizations banked on fickle human memories. Inverting Shakespeare's famous dialogue from *Julius Caesar*—"The evil that men do is oft interred with their bones."[12]— soiled reputations faded just as quickly from people's recall. Humans, after all, do not possess the memory of elephants, mammals renowned for their exceptional long-term memory (they possess among the largest brains in the animal kingdom)—until technology is introduced.

---

12 'Julius Caesar', William Shakespeare, produced in 1599–1600, published in 1623 from a transcript of a prompt book

The sophisticated nature of spurious content makes it nearly undetectable by humans. Technology offers the only solution to safeguard against deep fakes. Technology to combat technology. And technology remembers! Past transgressions of a brand or its parent company are etched into the system's memory and information repository. History cannot be erased. A plausible scenario is a 'trust index' that pops up whenever a brand or company attempts to communicate with you.

Imagine an advertisement for a sports shoe appearing on your laptop. Your AI system scans its historical records to highlight any deep fake or related incidents tied to the brand or company, globally. For example, a three-year-old promotional video in Mexico claimed the shoe's material was completely biodegradable. After testing, consumer activists exposed the claim as false, and the company vehemently denied creating the video. Your software flags the case, leaving you to decide whom to trust. Regardless of your decision, the important part is that it was brought to your attention, rather than buried in the pages of an old newspaper.

Darkness beyond deep fake?

While much of this discussion centers on external stakeholders, the concept of trust and protecting it from deep fakes also applies equally to internal interactions—between the organization and its employees, or between individual employees. A minor tweak to a celebrity video to portray the company in a positive light to employees may seem harmless and beneficial in the short term. However, once discovered, regaining trust becomes daunting.

The same principle applies to interactions with colleagues. Would you ever trust a co-worker again who once generated a fake email in your name?

JUMP-STARTING YOUR COMPANY

Safeguarding your company's reputation is critical in this new era where trust has evolved from a virtuous concept into a lever for competitive advantage. Consider the following pointers to protect your strategic edge:

1. Walk the talk

Thus far, trust—a staple in the company's value statement—has had minimal tangible impact on a firm's strategy. While progressive leaders and employees may disagree, this is the common belief. Given its newfound role as a competitive advantage, building and maintaining trust deserves serious attention. A single action by one employee can shatter that advantage. Therefore, it's essential to instill an understanding of trust as a strategic asset among all employees. Unwavering support from employees is crucial to retaining this edge. Shift 'trust' from a lofty value statement to operational action.

2. Red flag deep fake

Given the impressive outcomes deep fakes can deliver, the temptation to leverage them is immense. The justification may be that a small, 'innocent' embellishment isn't really a violation. However, 'small' is relative, and as audiences become more wary of manipulation, even the slightest breach can damage reputation. Vigilance is paramount both within the organization to prevent employees from creating deep fakes (either intentionally or not) and externally. Keep in mind, the organization takes the fall for any transgressions, even those not initiated by the company. This makes spotting deep fakes in cyberspace crucial—a task likely delegated to the firm's public relations agency. Tracking company references in formal media, identifying videos, images, or text mentioning the organization, and verifying their authenticity will become an additional responsibility for the team.

3. Institute a policy

Define the organization's stance on deep fakes. Establish a policy and disseminate it among employees. Involve the broader employee base in formulating the policy to gain buy-in. Moreover, the process of drafting the policy itself will provoke debate and sharpen understanding of acceptable boundaries.

4. Manage risk

To implement the policy, establish processes and security protocols, as well as graduated penalties for employees who violate the policy, depending on the severity of the offense. In light of the increasing prevalence of financial scams involving deep fakes, introduce multi-layered security verification procedures and encryption. Additionally, develop a crisis or contingency plan to handle the aftermath of inadvertent deep fakes or 'false flag' incidents.

JUMP-STARTING YOUR CAREER

While trust appears to be an organizational matter, a number of applications of deepfake target the individual employee.

The pointers below are aimed at shielding you, to ensure you are not victimized by deepfake sharks. At the same time, this is an area to which you could contribute—positively, of course!

1. Stay alert

Exploiting employees to scam an organization is the objective and modus operandi of many deepfake operations. The intent is to trick you into divulging corporate secrets, security measures, or even initiate unauthorized fund transfers. Trust your gut. The company's Chief Risk Management Officer asking for passwords on a video call? Or the Chief Financial Officer or Chief Executive Officer requesting a funds transfer to an unfamiliar external account? Definitely worth a double-check. Also, ensure you are up to date with the organization's security protocols.

2. Foster responsible action

As a responsible and invested employee, promote the importance of trust among colleagues. From your side, ensure you're perceived as a trusted team member.

3. Forge a circle of trust

External impressions are as vital as internal ones. Act with integrity when interacting with stakeholders—be they vendors, customers, board members, or others. While ethical conduct may have been ingrained in you early on, the difference now lies in being consciously aware of every action and conversation. A single misstep could lead to grave repercussions for you and your organization.

4. Ethical deep fake hacker

Mining deepfakes—for your organization or as a standalone career—is set to explode. It's an avenue worth exploring if you have the foundational knowledge and interest. Hone your skills, as ethical deepfake hackers are poised to become highly valued and well-compensated professionals.

CHAPTER 10

IQ
FOR WHOM THE BELLS TOLL

Generative AI is now in play,
IQ as a marker fades away,
With creativity in tow,
It's not what you know,
But how you adapt to the new day.

– ChatGPT, on being prompted to "create a limerick on generative artificial intelligence and the end of IQ as the sole indicator of success"[1]

---

1   Created and retrieved on 7 September 2024 2024

> *Empirical evidence demonstrates the fallacy of equating conventional, and often distorted, definitions of intelligence quotient (IQ) with success in the workplace. The Gen AI era further demolishes the IQ myth, harbingering, instead, a new set of competencies to thrive.*

THE RATIONALE
MALIGNED, YET RIDING HIGH

In the traditional paradigm, Intelligence Quotient (IQ) defined you, acting as a oracle of your likely achievements in school, admission to Ivy League-equivalent colleges, and success in the workplace. The higher the IQ, the higher and faster the ascent up the corporate ladder – or so classical wisdom declared.

IQ, a term coined by German-American psychologist Ludwig Wilhelm Stern in 1912 as an abbreviation and translation of the German *Intelligenzquotient*,[2] was devised to quantitatively measure an individual's cognitive ability. Over the years, numerous standardized tests have emerged, claiming to assess the constituent components of a person's intelligence: quantitative reasoning, verbal comprehension, spatial pattern recognition, processing speed, and other elements.

---

[2] 'The Intelligence Reflex', Indian Journal of Neurosciences, October – December 2017, 5658 (ijnonline.org) ; 'William Stern (1871–1938), Eclipsed Star of Early 20th-Century Psychology', Oxford Research Encyclopedias, 31 March 2020, William Stern (1871–1938), Eclipsed Star of Early 20th-Century Psychology | Oxford Research Encyclopedia of Psychology

Despite its prominence, the concept of IQ is controversial. Critics argue that these tests are culturally and socially biased, with content based on the experiences and knowledge of specific linguistic and socio-economic groups. Moreover, human intelligence is a complex, multifaceted concept that science still does not fully understand; reducing it to a single score is, at best, a naïve oversimplification. Many essential factors, such as creativity, problem-solving, and emotional intelligence, are not reflected in IQ assessments. Equating IQ with success is even more misguided, as it ignores the critical role of other factors like motivation, attitude, and social skills. Philosophers and psychologists pose a larger question: what defines success, and is there a single, universal definition?

Controversy aside, IQ remains popular in common parlance. Academic institutions and corporations continue to use the concept, albeit in a distorted form, as shorthand for preferred candidates. Entrance exams for top business schools measure applicants' ability to perform middle school mathematics, basic English grammar, and vocabulary. Similarly, many organizations in India follow this model, especially for entry-level management recruitment. Graduates from top-tier business schools—often viewed as proxies for "high IQ candidates"—are typically regarded as superior to those from lower-tier schools, leading to better roles, higher salaries, and generally being seen as high-potential recruits.

However, decades of empirical evidence suggest otherwise. A range of other skills, expertise, and behavioral traits contribute to success in the workplace. Average academic performers often turn out to be the ones who thrive in the long run. Look around: the majority of successful entrepreneurs were not class toppers. Yet, a few gold medallists have also risen to the top of the corporate pyramid. The reality is that relying on IQ tests for crystal-ball predictions of success is ineffective. Overwhelming evidence shows that IQ is not a reliable predictor of success.

A WHOLE NEW WORLD

Gen AI decisively shatters the myth. Mathematical computations, rules of grammar, word definitions, basic pattern recognition, and the like—Gen AI performs these tasks far faster than any human possibly could, with near-perfect accuracy. R.I.P., IQ as a barometer of individual progress in the workplace. Success in this epoch demands an entirely new set of competencies (some of which have been alluded to in the trends described thus far; here, we present a consolidated and comprehensive view).

1. Bend the spoon with your mind

The first wave of software, commercially deployed in India from the late 1980s to the end of the 1990s, rendered human involvement in data manipulation, basic analytics, and computations largely redundant. Computers were faster and free of human error. Soon, software advanced to handle increasingly complex analyses of massive datasets ('big data') and unstructured data (qualitative, not easily searchable, multi-format including text, audio, images, and video). Gen AI unleashed pattern recognition and the generation of guided creative output—two activities that were once the exclusive domain of humans: futurology and creativity.

Unsurprisingly, the brave new world no longer values rapid data analytics as a human skill. Can you solve 30 statistics problems in half an hour? Good for you—but rudimentary systems can do so in less than a second, making this a task for technology. Creativity, once considered the ultimate human bastion—irrespective of how smart or powerful machines became—was thought to be untouchable. Gen AI is now nibbling at the edges of this belief, creating text, audio, and visual output based on patterns from representative human work.

Assume you're the marketing head for biscuits at your company. Say goodbye to the tedious hours spent poring over sales data and crunching numbers for market insights. Not only does the system analyze the data, but it also presents conclusions in plain language, complete with recommended actions. Another time-consuming activity—communicating with colleagues to issue instructions and share updates—is handled by Gen AI, which drafts emails in your style, with nuanced language designed to elicit a positive response. A revised advertisement copy arrives for your review; the system even shares an assessment of its effectiveness. You turn your attention to the future, but the technology is one step ahead—having already scanned market trends and social media chatter to suggest new biscuit variants your company could launch.

This begs the question: what is your value-add to the organization? Technology appears to be performing your tasks—many of them, but not all. In this emerging reality, where all obvious or logical paths are charted by Gen AI, only an offbeat idea adds meaningful value. Consequently, lateral thinking to generate maverick solutions becomes the new-age competency for success.

Lateral thinking, a term coined by Maltese psychologist Edward de Bono in 1967, refers to approaching a problem from unusual perspectives to arrive at an innovative, non-conventional solution—one that cannot be deduced through normal logical reasoning. For clarity, divergent thinking, a related term, is a broader concept aimed at mapping multiple ideas without running them through a feasibility test.[3] Lateral thinking takes this further, narrowing down to a unique, workable, unorthodox solution. A line from *The Matrix* superbly exemplifies the mindset:

> *Young Monk: "Do not try and bend the spoon—that's impossible. Instead, only try to realize the truth."*
> *Neo: "What truth?"*
> *Young Monk: "There is no spoon."*

Until recently, out-of-the-box thinking served as fodder for bestsellers, while most organizations—when candid—admitted they were more comfortable with conventional thinkers. Their ideas, and even the individuals themselves, fit better within organizational culture. Now, with lateral thinking becoming a mainstream competency, organizations will need to choose between 'fit' and 'survival.'

2. Drive a tractor wearing *bindi*

Increased adoption and reliance on Gen AI and related technologies has spurred the democratization of knowledge and data-driven insights. Ubiquitous access to information and easy availability of automated advanced analytics negates

---

[3] 'Lateral thinking', Interaction Design Foundation website, What is Lateral Thinking? — updated 2024 | IxDF (interaction-design.org)

their value as levers of competitive advantage, heightening the significance of other elements to derive a strategic edge.

A deep understanding of existing and potential customers, and the nuances of their lives beyond the obvious, is a potent differentiator. There are plenty of examples of companies tweaking global or generic products to suit regional preferences and restrictions. One of the most commonly cited is McDonald's replacing its classic beef burger with chicken, and introducing vegetarian options like a potato-based burger for India. Lay's, the potato chips brand, localized even further—drawing on pappadam traditions, it launched wafer-style chips in flavours such as 'salt with pepper' and 'sundried chilli' to cater to South Indian tastes.[4] *Sairat*, the box-office Marathi hit (with early morning and midnight shows added to meet demand), offers a striking example of societal complexity.[5] Archana, the wealthy heroine, drives a tractor through her sugarcane field—an act commonly seen as feisty or bratty. But those familiar with hyper-local society know that in many agricultural communities of Maharashtra, unlike much of India, women do take on traditionally male roles. As Nagraj Manjule, the film's director, puts it, "The strong, independent women in the villages around me were

---

4   'Here's how Lay's is transforming its products with evolving consumer preferences', Business Insider, 13 September 2021, Here's how Lay's is transforming its products with evolving consumer preferences | Business Insider India

5   'Sairat: Why a doomed love story has become India's sleeper hit', BBC News, 7 June 2016, Sairat: Why a doomed love story has become India's sleeper hit - BBC News ; 'Sairat' in Marathi translates to 'Wild'

inspirations for the female lead." Advertising targeted at women tractor drivers, anyone?

With the race to develop the next culturally resonant product or message heating up, a one-off or superficial inspiration won't cut it. A systemic, expert-driven approach to glean and apply cultural or behavioural norms becomes crucial. Sociologists, anthropologists, and psychologists now play a pivotal role—becoming core team members. Expect a radical overhaul of team structures: behavioural scientists and culture aficionados, once outsiders, enter the mainstream. And the baseline of cultural sensitivity and societal awareness—even for non-behavioural roles—soars.

As the relevance of IQ fades, the importance of cultural quotient grows.

3. "I feel you"

Empathy is the new ambrosia—the mythical drink of the Greek gods conferring immortality—serving multiple strategic purposes today. Once perceived as a weakness, emotional quotient has become a strength in the Gen AI era.

Empathy fuels cultural understanding and helps build personal rapport. As mentioned earlier, societal awareness enables organizations to stand out. Ironically, in an age of sophisticated technology, it's relationships and the human factor that become decisive differentiators. When the playing field is level or choices are complex, people do business with those they know and trust. Fellowship and bonding tip the scale.

The ability to connect with diverse co-workers is equally crucial. Inclusivity isn't a passing fad; it's a growing priority, with the baseline rising steadily. Gen AI brings in a new mix of experts with varied mindsets—mavericks, sociologists, super-specialists, and others. Integrating these groups and navigating the complex dynamics that follow demands high emotional intelligence.

Gen AI marks the decline of hyper-macho culture and the rise of the 'I feel you'[6] era.

4. Living on the edges[7]

With deep technologies executing many tasks traditionally undertaken by humans—often better than people—and with the capability to take on more, the human role is shifting from hands-on execution to strategic oversight. This change is evident across organizational hierarchies and functions. Gen AI and its ilk, shouldering increasing responsibility, free up the human manager, allowing her/him to take on additional duties.

Take Sreelatha[8], a worker in a garment manufacturing facility. Her sole task was marking fabric as per the set pattern and size. Automation and the use of software such as CAD advanced Sreelatha to a supervisory role, overseeing fabric marking and cutting. As technology evolved, manual sewing was eliminated. Sophisticated machinery and software now act as an intermediary supervisory layer, freeing up more of Sreelatha's time. Ambitious, hard-working, and a quick learner, she now also oversees sewing and finishing. Before

---

6 Present day slang for expressing empathy with someone
7 Paraphrased from 1993 Aerosmith's song 'Livin' on the edge'
8 Hypothetical name and situation

long, the entire operation is automated. Sreelatha transitions from performing a single operational task to managing the entire assembly line.

Routine duties now revolve around monitoring output parameters. The only substantial human role is problem-solving, in the rare instance of a glitch. Gen AI, combined with other advanced technologies, can resolve many of these. Moreover, ensuring adherence to output parameters and taking corrective action is steadily becoming system-led. Given this, Sreelatha could conceivably manage multiple assembly lines—and take on dispatch responsibilities.

This expanding span of control demands a commensurate width of knowledge, sparking the resurgence of the generalist.

Conversely, domain experts will be required to train systems or carry out specialised activities: researchers developing a life-longevity drug, sociologists mapping the buying behaviour of middle-class college girls in tier-2 cities in Telangana, sculptors envisaging their next exhibition. The current corporate definition of 'expert' is somewhat elastic, with many consultancies dubbing employees 'experts' after (literally!) a three-month assignment. Gen AI, driven by the democratisation of knowledge, tightens the standards—denoting either a doctoral degree or decades of hands-on experience.

The imminent era belongs to generalists and blue-blood specialists.

5. Connecting the dots

Divine epiphanies aside, out-of-the-box ideas usually emerge from juxtaposing knowledge across diverse areas. Layering cricket trivia with music theory and valuation techniques can spur a Eureka moment.

Scientific inventions are full of such stories. In 1941, George de Mestral returned from a hunting trip with his Irish Pointer.[9] He noticed burrs from a burdock plant stuck to both him and his dog. Curiosity piqued: there was no glue on the burrs, so how did they stick? Under the microscope, he discovered thousands of tiny hooks that allowed binding to fabric and animal skin. He created a synthetic version—voila, Velcro was born.

Another tale is that of the Japanese bullet trains. Travelling between 240 and 320 kilometres per hour and carting millions of passengers annually, the Shinkansen is a boon to citizens.[10] But early versions hit a snag. High speeds caused pressure waves at the front of the train, creating a deafening 'tunnel boom' that disturbed nearby residents. Engineers took inspiration from kingfisher birds—known for their silent dives into water—to redesign the train. This not only eliminated the tunnel boom but also led to a 10 per cent increase in speed and a 15 per cent reduction in electricity use.

In addition to wide-ranging interests, the ability to connect the dots is crucial. While similar to seeing the big

---

9 'An Idea That Stuck: How George de Mestral Invented the VELCRO® Brand Fastener', Velcro website, 11 November 2016, An Idea That Stuck: How George de Mestral Invented the Velcro Fastener ; 'George de Mestral', Creative Huddle website, George de Mestral | Creative Huddle

10 'The Shinkansen bullet train from JR-West', AskNature website, High Speed Train Inspired by the Kingfisher — Innovation — AskNature

picture, this skill blends interdisciplinary knowledge and lateral (or creative) thinking. Insights from one area are rarely transferable as-is. Transposing experiences across domains requires imagination—the ability to take a nugget of learning that's out of context and make it fit elsewhere. Cross-pollination of knowledge is the new strategic advantage.

6. Problem formulation

The more advanced the technology, the more complex it is to use—or so the adage goes. Gen AI dispels this belief, achieving new heights in being human-friendly and intuitive. Still, technology is technology, and the decades-old maxim 'garbage in, garbage out' holds true. Clear instructions yield superior results, making problem-statement formulation a critical competency. Defining objectives, boundary conditions, and parameters tightly and unambiguously equips the system to deliver an appropriate response. Corporate professionals—particularly management consultants—pride themselves on mastering this skill.

However, Gen AI compels a rethink of the traditional approach to crafting problem statements. Conventional frameworks, characterised by rigidity and delineation, often drive systems toward the most predictable, well-trodden logical answer.

Such an approach would have yielded a response of 'a faster horse,' denying the world the Ford Model T and the automobile revolution—or at least postponing it.[11] Streaming

---

11 'On Building A Faster Horse: Design Thinking For Disruption', Forbes, 19 October 2017. On Building A Faster Horse: Design Thinking For Disruption (forbes.com)

services, the dominant entertainment delivery mode of this era, provide another illustration of moving beyond orthodox problem definitions. As recently as the early 2000s, consumers rented DVDs (or earlier, VHS tapes) to watch movies. Netflix, instead of pursuing the obvious answer—'a faster, cheaper, more convenient DVD rental service'—took a leap of faith by launching content streaming in 2007.[12] Challenges abounded: low broadband penetration, consumer attachment to physical ownership, and aggressive tactics from DVD rental rivals. Yet Netflix chose to ignore the straight-and-narrow path.

The inflexible, tightly bound problem-statement technique disregards the potential of creative employees—or Gen AI—to build on existing ideas. Problem-solving in the emerging paradigm is no longer a linear process. Mirroring this shift, problem formulation now demands latitude and fluid boundaries, allowing for expansive, out-of-the-box thinking. Expect an iterative process that generates diverse outputs, which can then be synthesised into more nuanced and impactful solutions. In the final analysis, this new-age approach delivers outcomes that are significantly more innovative and compelling.

JUMP-STARTING YOUR COMPANY

Instilling new competencies in employees is the litmus test of truly taking the team along. Without buy-in from

---

[12] 'Digital Disrupt: What Businesses Can Learn From Netflix', Business.com, 24 July 2024, What Small Businesses Can Learn From Netflix ; 'Leading through Disruption: Netflix as the Disruptive Leader', Bold Narratives, 12 May 2023, Leading through Disruption: Netflix as the Disruptive Leader (boldnarratives.com)

all constituencies and strong execution of the training programme, even the most elaborate plans will fall flat.

1. Set the stage

While Gen AI may be a popular buzzword among your company's employees, shareholders, and board members ('the extended team'), its full implications are not evident to most. Navigating the imminent wave of disruption demands a new playbook of competencies. Successfully making these sharp changes—in skills and mindset—will only be possible with the extended team's full support and commitment. Begin by aligning on the need to reassess the future-fit value of each competency.

2. Identify fit-for-purpose competencies

The new-age competencies discussed earlier in this chapter apply broadly across organizations, but their relative relevance varies depending on the unique context of the firm and role. Each position demands its own distinct DNA of competencies. For instance, the depth of knowledge and experience required from a branding specialist in a marketing advisory firm is different from that in a construction company. Similarly, 'connecting the dots' is core to strategy roles, whereas operational positions prioritize efficient execution over abstract thinking.

There may also be specialist competencies specific to your context that aren't covered here.

3. Design training programmes

Once the relevant competencies for each role are identified, swiftly design customized reskilling or upskilling programmes for every employee. This urgency stems from two realities: Gen AI is already here, and reskilling always takes longer than anticipated.

The new-age skills represent a sharp break—not a natural extension—of earlier competencies. This reflects the Gen AI transformation: discontinuous, not incremental change. In some cases, in-house training may suffice; in others, formal academic courses will be necessary. Brace your company for the next-level commitment required for reskilling—sabbaticals, learning breaks, or reduced working hours to carve out time for study.

4. Review recruitment plans

Many new competencies may be difficult or inefficient to develop in-house. Take expertise in nano materials, for example. While the company could hire a science graduate and invest heavily in their development over 5–7 years to produce a PhD in advanced materials, recruiting an existing expert is far quicker and more sensible. As a secondary benefit, inducting fresh talent sparks new thinking, which aligns well with the evolving context.

5. Re-calibrate evaluation parameters

Reskilling existing employees or recruiting new talent is the first step toward bridging the competency gap. Appropriate rewards and incentives must be introduced to retain talent and encourage the team to further hone their skills. Since the new competencies differ drastically from those previously valued, a complete overhaul of the performance evaluation framework and metrics is needed.

JUMP-STARTING YOUR CAREER

Buckle up: the burden of action in this trend falls squarely on you. While organizations can create an enabling environment and provide opportunities, the onus of reskilling rests squarely on your shoulders. In the competitive job market, staying ahead of the curve is your responsibility.

1. Map yourself

Reconstruct your current role, and the promotion position you've been eyeing, through the Gen AI lens to determine the new set of competencies required to thrive. Assess your capabilities and interest level to fill the skill gaps. Ask yourself: are you truly equipped and excited to reskill as required? Picture this: your redefined role entails comprehending the concepts of finance – a discipline you've historically found boring and steered clear of. Alternatively, your role 2.0 might demand specialism in food chemistry, a field out of your comfort zone.

On the other hand, your familiarity with classic English movies may be a huge bonus as your role, in the Gen AI era, widens to include film content curation. This is a time of transformative change, with organizational structure and roles being remodeled. In this milieu of upheaval, organizations are more receptive than ever to reassigning responsibilities. Grab the opportunity to reinvent yourself!

2. Skill yourself

Take charge of your future! Having identified the competencies you need to develop, get to it. Don't bank on your organization; treat assistance from your company as a bonus. Sign up for appropriate courses proactively. With the plethora of flexi-study and online programmes available, you should be able to find a relevant option.

3. Rebuild yourself

A short-term workshop may not suffice for all knowledge enhancement or reskilling endeavors. Instead, a full-time one-year or even multi-year course may be required. As the bar for specialists rises, opting for a long-duration PhD or equivalent programme will become more common. Undertaking a sabbatical of this nature entails careful planning to manage finances for fees and prepare for a period of minimal or no income.

In the words of the famous British writer, C. S. Lewis, "Hardships often prepare ordinary people for an extraordinary destiny." The effort you put in and the hurdles you overcome now should transform you professionally from a caterpillar to a butterfly.

CHAPTER 11

BRING YOUR AVATAR TO WORK

In the workplace, AI's on the rise,
Crafting avatars, sleek and wise.
They chat and they grin,
Never tiring of spin,
Bringing work with a digital guise!

– ChatGPT, on being prompted to "create a limerick on generative artificial intelligence and Avatars in the workplace"[1]

---

1 Created and retrieved on 28 August 2024

> *Gen AI, combined with deep technologies such as Extended Reality and Holograms, will revolutionize the way we interact with colleagues. Expect clone-like avatars to take your place in meetings. Powered by Gen AI, your avatar will mimic your responses, facial expressions, and gestures, during official discussions. Sounds like science-fiction, but this reality is closer than assumed.*

THE RATIONALE

I AM HERE; YET I AM NOT

COVID-19 accelerated the acceptance and adoption of remote working, plausibly by nearly two decades. Initial acquiescence gave way to the recognition of the tremendous value of work-from-anywhere.

Lifestyle-friendly perks and savings on commuting costs are the obvious benefits. From an organizational perspective, 'teleporting' expertise probably ranks as the number one advantage. Specialists – whether bankers, doctors, or professionals from any other field – can be leveraged, regardless of their geographic location. The world authority on dinosaur-age paleontology, residing in Ottawa, Canada, can teach and inspire a group of students located 75 kilometers outside Aizawl. Combined with the right equipment, the concept of remote operations has a groundbreaking impact on human safety. Functioning in physically hazardous or hostile environments – such as mines, outer space, underwater, and volcano-prone areas – has been rendered largely risk-free.

Currently, Zoom, Teams, and similar applications enable virtual meetings. Gen AI, integrated with frontier technologies, is catalyzing the next generation of remote work, opening up mind-bending possibilities. These science fiction-like scenarios are not just fantasies; they are real and here to stay.

Poetically put: I am here; yet, I am not.

TECHNOLOGIES THAT MATTER

First, a brief primer on some of the more advanced (or 'deep' in tech parlance) technologies that, in conjunction with Gen AI, will reshape how we interact at work. Please note that the list below is not comprehensive.

Extended Reality (XR) encompasses Virtual Reality (VR), Augmented Reality (AR), and Mixed Reality (MR). VR sits at one end of the spectrum, creating an immersive, fictitious digital environment. AR, on the other hand, overlays digital content on the real-world physical reality. The virtual elements (graphics, sound, etc.) evolve in response to the user's actions and changes in the physical environment. Think of VR as a purely fictitious world, whereas AR is part fiction and part reality. MR lies between VR and AR on the spectrum, blending a digital reproduction of the physical world with fictitious digital elements.

Unlike holograms and similar technologies (discussed later), auxiliary devices such as glasses or headsets, controllers, and smartphones are required to experience XR.

Hologram technology creates a stereographic, three-dimensional, life-sized doppelganger of a real-world physical object or person using principles of light interference. Spectators can walk around the image, viewing it from all angles, without wearing special glasses or equipment. Real-time actions of users are transmitted and transferred to their holograms, subject to the availability of high bandwidth (typically 5G or 6G) and low latency time. Holograms are generally considered more realistic than Augmented Reality.

While holograms check the visual box, simulating touch – known as haptics technology in scientific lingo – remains the key missing element. Not for long, though. Researchers at various universities are working on creating touchable or tactile holograms using ultrasound emitters.[2]

Building on holographic technology is telepresence – simulating physical presence at a remote location, either virtually or via robotic avatars.[3] **Telepresence robots**, equipped with video cameras, microphones, screens, and speakers, enable the user to maintain a 'physical' presence in a remote location. For instance, a specialist cardiac surgeon seated in Mumbai can 'participate in' and advise her colleagues performing a complex open-heart surgery in Dhanbad,

---

2 'Holograms You Can Touch and Feel', Science Connected, 23 January 2024, Holograms You Can Touch and Feel - Science Connected Magazine ; 'Researchers uncover physical limitation in haptic holography', UC Santa Barbara website, 1 March 2023, Researchers uncover physical limitation in haptic holography | The Current (ucsb.edu)

3 'A Perspective on Robotic Telepresence and Teleoperation using Cognition: Are we there yet', arxiv website, 2022, https://arxiv.org/pdf/2203.02959 ; 'Telepresence robot', TechTarget website, What is a Telepresence Robot? | Definition from TechTarget

Jharkhand. The next stage, teleoperation, allows for real-world interaction at the target venue. Located in landlocked Kharagpur, an engineer can undertake repairs to a deep-sea cable in the Central Basin of the Indian Ocean, without risking a dive into an 8,000-plus feet deep environment.

Spatial audio mimics the way humans perceive sound in real-life settings, accounting for variations in pitch, volume, and reverberation levels of sound.[4] Importantly, the technology is direction-sensitive. If a speaker is standing in front of you and you turn right, your right ear will pick up slightly, but perceptibly, more of their words than your left ear. Spatial audio technology replicates this effect. Likewise, sounds from above or behind you also play out differently. Spatial audio can be 'object-based,' where the sound is built into the object emitting the sound, or ambisonic, where the sound is centered around the listener. Current spatial audio technology already allows for individualization, factoring in the listener's head measurements and the distance between the ears. This contrasts with its precursor, 3D audio, which not only lacked the potential for personalization but also provided an immersive sound experience only in a specific spot in a room.

Interacting with these technologies creates a new world – the **Metaverse**, a term coined by American science fiction

---

[4] 'New VR Tech Aims to Take Surround-Sound to the Next Level', Scientific American, 17 October 2017, New VR Tech Aims to Take Surround-Sound to the Next Level | Scientific American ; 'What is spatial audio?', Qualcomm website, 16 November 2020, What is Spatial Audio | Advanced 3D Audio Technology | Qualcomm

author Neal Stephenson in his 1992 novel *Snow Crash*.[5] While formal definitions vary across academics and researchers, the Metaverse is broadly defined as a collective virtual open space, integrating physically persistent virtual reality with virtually enhanced physical reality.[6] For the non-geeks, 'physically persistent' refers to the applicability of the ordinary principles of the physical world. For instance, if an object is moved from location A to location B, the next time you enter the Metaverse, you'll still find the object in location B. 'Virtually enhanced physical reality' refers to superimposing digital elements, such as animation, over a digital version of the physical world.

The platform generates a virtual parallel or 'digital twin' of the physical world, free from real world limitation, much like Augmented Reality. Often colloquially tagged as web 4.0, the Metaverse encompasses real-time interactions between users, devices, and data. While the Metaverse was the buzzword a year or so ago, it has since lost steam.

---

5   'Snow Crash', Neal Stephenson, first published in 1992 by Bantam Books

6   'The Metaverse: Innovations and generative AI', Science Direct, September 2023, The Metaverse: Innovations and generative AI - ScienceDirect ; 'Metaverse as a disruptive technology revolutionising tourism management and marketing', Science Direct, August 2023, Metaverse as a disruptive technology revolutionising tourism management and marketing - ScienceDirect ; 'Metaverse and Generative AI: Envisioning the Future of Human-Computer Interaction', 7 November 2023, S&P Global website, Metaverse & Generative AI in Future | S&P Global (spglobal.com)

Quantum communication addresses a fundamental concern of all virtual interactions: security. Hackers are inevitably a few steps ahead of encryption experts! However, at least theoretically, interception or eavesdropping on quantum communication is impossible without leaving behind a trace of the act. Based on the principles of quantum physics, data is transmitted through light photons – called quantum bits or qubits – over optical cables.[7] Any attempt to observe the qubits in transit, let alone alter them, results in the collapse of the immensely fragile qubits, immediately alerting the users.

CASTLES IN THE (DIGITAL) SKY?

Exciting as these technologies appear, are they pipe dreams – possibilities that are at least half a century away? The future is arriving faster than you think, though admittedly, each technology is at a varying stage of evolution.

Mature technologies: virtual reality, augmented reality, spatial audio

At the 'mature' end of the scale lie **Virtual Reality** and **Augmented Reality**. 'Mature' is a relative term – neither VR nor AR is remotely as established as mobile telephony.

Gamers have embraced VR and AR since the 1980s. *No Man's Sky*, a fully immersive VR experience, creates a spectacular adventure-filled universe for the user. Players battle aliens, explore new planets, and tumble through adventures as they attempt to reach the center of the universe. *Half-Life:*

---

[7] 'Explainer: What is quantum communication?', 14 February 2019, MIT Technology Review, Explainer: What is quantum communication? | MIT Technology Review

Alyx and *Beat Saber* are just a few of the 4,000-plus VR games currently on the market. On the AR front, *Pokémon Go* had players using their phone's GPS to locate, capture, train, and battle virtual Pokémons in real-world settings. This legendary AR-based game sparked a worldwide frenzy. Norway's then Prime Minister, Erna Solberg, was caught playing *Pokémon Go* during a parliamentary debate, and again while on an official visit to Slovakia.[8] Taiwan issued a staggering 350 fines in a single day to motorcyclists playing mid-ride.[9]

In the corporate arena, VR is no longer a novelty. A host of companies use VR extensively for employee training and digital twinning (creating a virtual model of a physical object or space). VR simulates a wide range of scenarios, preparing employees to navigate various, often challenging, situations. "Immersive learning allows us to recreate those situations that we can't or don't want to recreate at the store with customers present," says Andy Trainor, Vice President of US Learning at Walmart.[10] In addition, switching from in-person to immersive learning slashed training time by a whopping 96 per cent for Walmart, from 8 hours to a mere 15 minutes.

---

8   'Norway's PM caught playing Pokémon Go in parliament', The Guardian, 5 October 2016, Norway's PM caught playing Pokémon Go in parliament | Pokémon Go | The Guardian

9   'Hundreds of Pokémon Go players fined for playing while driving in Taiwan', The Guardian, 8 August 2016, Hundreds of Pokémon Go players fined for playing while driving in Taiwan | Pokémon Go | The Guardian

10 'Walmart cuts training time by 96 per cent with immersive learning', Strivr website, Strivr helps Walmart reduce training time by 96 per cent | Customer story

Post-training employee assessment scores jumped by 10–15 per cent compared to non-VR learners. Closer to home, Tata Motors uses VR for virtual prototyping—assessing features from design to safety, including the placement of critical occupant restraint systems like seatbelts and airbags.[11]

Augmented Reality (AR) is firmly entrenched in the business world. Numerous global and Indian brands are leveraging AR to elevate customer experience—allowing users model clothes, accessories, or beauty products before buying, without waiting in serpentine queues outside the trial room. Companies like Nykaa, the e-commerce beauty products brand, deploy this technology to offer virtual try-ons for customers.[12] Many of us have toiled for hours dragging furniture across rooms, only to realize that the earlier layout looked better. These struggles are becoming a thing of the past. Leveraging a combination of AR and VR, Ikea allows users to virtually arrange (and rearrange many, many times over!) the furniture placement in their homes.[13] Moving from services to manufacturing, Bharat Forge, a leader in forgings,

---

11 'Beyond Aesthetics, How Auto Designers Fuse Safety and Design in Vehicle Renders', Tata Motors website, 12 July 2023, Beyond Aesthetics, How Auto Designers Fuse Safety and Design in Vehicle Renders - Tata Motors

12 '5 Examples of Brands Using AR/VR Retail to Enhance Their Digital E-commerce Capabilities', Mayura Consultancy Services, 17 August 2021, AR/VR in Retail: 5 Brands enhancing Ecommerce capability (mayuraconsultancy.com)

13 'Retail Trends: 5 Companies using AI/AR tools to enhance customer experience', Indian Retailing, 3 August 2023, Retail Trends: 5 Companies using AI/AR tools to enhance customer experience (indiaretailing.com)

uses AR to train and guide operators during the maintenance process.[14] Porsche employs AR for virtual collaboration between dealership technicians and remote experts for live interactions, shortening service resolution times by up to 40 per cent.[15]

Although use cases for AR and VR continue to multiply and become more mainstream, some hurdles linger. These technologies require auxiliary equipment, such as headsets. Over time, these devices will likely become ubiquitous and part of one's everyday trousseau, much like mobile phones. A few users complain of motion sickness resulting from extended headset usage. The overall verdict: a few challenges persist, but the technologies are very much here and now.

Related to VR and AR is spatial audio—another "mature" technology. Increasingly, virtual meeting platforms such as Microsoft Teams integrate spatial audio to offer an immersive experience.[16] A few ultra-luxurious Mercedes-Maybach models embed spatial audio technologies into their in-car infotainment system.[17]

---

14 'Bharat Forge Annual Report 2020 – 21', Bharat Forge website, Manufactured Capital (bharatforge.com)

15 'Porsche Announces Augmented Reality at Scale, Powered by Atheer', IoTone website, Porsche Announces Augmented Reality at Scale, Powered by Atheer by Atheer | IoT ONE Digital Transformation Advisors

16 'Spatial audio in Microsoft Teams meetings', Microsoft website, Spatial audio in Microsoft Teams meetings - Microsoft Support

17 'Apple, Mercedes-Benz partner to bring Spatial Audio to different models', Business Standard, 17 October 2022, Apple, Mercedes-

Emerging technologies: mixed reality, hologram, telepresence robots

Mixed Reality, a hybrid of VR and AR, unlike its constituent elements, is at a relatively nascent stage of adoption—an "emerging technology." That said, early adopters have started incorporating the technology into their operations. Porsche leverages MR for product demonstrations and technical briefings.[18] Users interact with virtual objects and other participants from remote locations around the globe. Additionally, they can engage with their real-world surroundings, enabling them to take notes or check their phones. Reliance Jio, anticipating a meteoric rise in demand, launched MR glasses Jio Glass—which can be connected to a smartphone, computer, or gaming console.[19] L&T Construction uses VR and AR, along with a smattering of MR, to train employees on safety practices in daunting scenarios—heights, excavation sites, dangerous or hazardous materials, and high-tension lines, among others.[20] Project visualization is another application.

Benz partner to bring Spatial Audio to different models | Technology News - Business Standard (business-standard.com)

18 'Immersive presentations: how Porsche is stepping into mixed reality', Porsche website, 17 January 2024, Immersive presentations: how Porsche is stepping into mixed reality - Porsche Newsroom

19 'Reliance Jio unveils mixed reality 'JioGlass' smart glass', Economic Times Telecom, 31 October 2023, Reliance Jio unveils mixed reality 'JioGlass' smart glass, ET Telecom (indiatimes.com)

20 'Building a Safety Culture', L&T website, Building a Safety Culture | Technology for Growth | L&T (larsentoubro.com) ;

Despite its high-visibility status, **holograms** also fall into the "emerging" technology category. Prime Minister Modi's election rallies in 2012 and 2013 are perhaps the most notable illustration of hologram technology in India. He created a Guinness World Record during the 2012 Gujarat assembly elections by simultaneously addressing 53 locations across 25 cities in the state.[21] Modi replicated the "simultaneous, multi-location presence" strategy during his 2014 General Elections campaign across numerous cities. Hyderabad, for example, played host to 15 in-city holographic locations.[22]

In 2018, the first 5G hologram call took place between England and Manchester City Women's Football Captain, Steph Houghton, and a young fan, Iris.[23] Following its success, telecom operators Deutsche Telekom, Orange, Telefónica, and Vodafone, along with Matsuko—the world's first holographic presence app—piloted an easy-to-make holographic call.[24]

ECC Concord, in-house journal of L&T Construction, Special issue on Digitalization, concord_jan17.pdf (Intecc.com)

21 'BJP spent Rs 60 crore on Narendra Modi's 3D rallies during Lok Sabha polls', The Times of India, 21 January 2025, BJP spent Rs 60 crore on Narendra Modi's 3D rallies during Lok Sabha polls | India News - Times of India (indiatimes.com)

22 Modi set to arrive in Hyderabad along with his holograms' The Times of India, 5 August 2013, Modi set to arrive in Hyderabad along with his holograms | Hyderabad News - Times of India (indiatimes.com)

23 'Vodafone makes UK's first holographic call using 5G', Vodafone website, 20 September 2018, Vodafone makes UK's first holographic call using 5G

24 'Deutsche Telekom, Orange, Telefónica and Vodafone together with Matsuko implement a proof of concept of holographic

Users simply made a phone call to join a shared holographic communication session.

Despite its obvious convenience over all forms of Extended Reality—no bulky headsets or wearable gear required—hologram adoption lags behind AR and VR. Bandwidth limitations, complexity, and cost remain key hurdles. But the imminent roll-out of 5G and 6G networks shifts the equation: high bandwidth and low latency will dramatically boost quality. At the same time, advances in capturing and rendering hardware, including projection technology, will ease deployment complexity. Finally, as with all technologies, increased usage will drive down costs.

Surprisingly, **telepresence robots** still sit in the emerging technology category. While robotics are now widespread in the corporate world and no longer considered a novelty, the at-scale commercial application of telepresence robots—where a person remotely controls the movements of a machine—remains limited. Theoretical constructs and even pilot runs of surgeons performing procedures remotely have been well-documented. However, prerequisites like stable internet connectivity with low latency hinder the mainstream adoption of the technology. For example, an unexpected 10 per cent drop in internet speed could spell disaster for a patient.

Another dampener is the rapid progress in adjacent technologies. Integrating AI into robots enables full

---

presence as a simple phone call', Vodafone website, 21 September 2022, Vodafone and partners implement trial for holographic calls ; 'The creation of MATSUKO, the world's first holographic presence app', Matsuko website, Team Page (matsuko.com)

automation, eliminating the need for human guidance and, consequently, reducing the need for telepresence robots.

Experimental technologies: quantum communication

Research institutions are working on developing and refining quantum communications. In 2016, China established the world's first trunk line (physical fiber cable) for secure quantum telecommunications—a 2,000-kilometer link between Beijing and Shanghai.[25] Chinese businesses such as Bank of Communications, the Industrial and Commercial Bank of China, and Alibaba use the network.

In terms of free-space transmission (through the atmosphere without the use of physical cables), several early trials are underway, notably the 3,800-kilometer link between a ground station near Moscow and one at Urumqi in China's western Xinjiang region.[26] Leveraging Mozi, China's quantum satellite, two images encoded and secured by quantum keys were successfully transmitted between the two locations.

India, too, is poised to become a pioneer in this field. In March 2020, the Indian Space Research Organisation

---

25 'China Opens 2,000-km Quantum Communication Line', ICBC website, China Opens 2,000-km Quantum Communication Line-Home-ICBC China (icbkus.com) ; 'Quantum leap for hack-proof communication recorded by ISRO-SAC', The Times of India, 29 March 2021, Ahmedabad: Quantum leap for hack-proof communication recorded by Isro-SAC | Ahmedabad News - Times of India (indiatimes.com)

26 'Report: China and Russia Test Quantum Communication Link', The Quantum Insider, 2 January 2024, Report: China and Russia Test Quantum Communication Link (thequantuminsider.com)

(ISRO) demonstrated the country's capabilities in the field by showcasing free-space quantum communication over a 300-meter distance.[27] Encouraged by this success, ISRO partnered with the Physical Research Laboratory (PRL) to further advance quantum communication technology, which will eventually be integrated into an ISRO-built quantum satellite.

While early trials have been successful, several critical impediments hinder broader adoption of quantum communication—chief among them are maintaining the stability of quantum signals over long distances, line-of-sight limitations, and the need for complex, advanced infrastructure.

THE TALE OF AVENGERS

Much like Iron Man, Captain America, Hulk, Thor, Black Widow, and Hawkeye join forces to form an invincible squad capable of vanquishing Thanos, integrating Gen AI into the technologies mentioned above revolutionizes the way we work.

Imagine this scenario: It's 9:25 am on a chilly winter weekday morning, with the snow-covered Himalayas in

---

27 'Department of Space demonstrates entanglement based quantum communication over 300m free space along with real time cryptographic applications', ISRO website, Department of Space demonstrates entanglement based quantum communication over 300m free space along with real time cryptographic applications (isro.gov.in) ; 'ISRO aims to launch QKD satellite, Ahmedabad to play key role', The Economic Times Telecom, 24 June 2023, Indian Space Research Organisation: ISRO aims to launch QKD satellite, Ahmedabad to play key role, ET Telecom (indiatimes.com)

the backdrop. You're snuggled under a duvet in a bed-and-breakfast in Leh, while your weekly update meeting starts in five minutes in the boardroom of your company's head office in Gurgaon. Amazingly, your boss is completely at ease, confident that you'll attend the meeting.

Extended Reality and holograms make this possible by generating a life-sized 3D avatar of you, even placing you in your favorite seat in the boardroom. In fact, the quality of your image is so lifelike that, as people walk into the room, they struggle to tell if it's you in person or just your avatar. Spatial audio ensures that your words emanate from your avatar, whether seated or walking around the room, not a speaker planted at the center of the board table.

Now, add a touch of Gen AI to create potent outcomes. Based on your past responses, Gen AI could mimic your reactions and your unique style of phrasing in the ensuing conversation. To everyone present, you (your avatar, actually!) jump in at appropriate moments in the discussion, offering comments just as you would. Gen AI's memory, analytical power, and network linkage identification capabilities are the cherry on top.

Siddhartha, the product development lead, commits to showcasing the prototype of the new motorcycle model by the 5th of next month. Sans Gen AI, you'd be rummaging through your meeting notes to check whether his timeline has remained consistent. Heaven forbid, if you can't find your notes—or worse, forgot to take any. No such snag with a Gen AI-enabled avatar; 'you' calmly point out that Siddhartha had earlier mentioned a deadline in the third week of this month and that the delay is unacceptable.

Next up: Amit, your finance person, drones through a series of figures, arguing that the new motorcycle model is economically unviable at the proposed price. On the slim chance that you manage to stay awake through Amit's monotone monologue and alert enough to follow the numbers—then perform mental mathematical gymnastics within seconds—you might just catch an error. Your avatar, of course, handles all three tasks effortlessly.

Proactively, Gen AI maps out the linkages in Amit's analysis, much like plotting moves in a chess game. Scaling up the new motorcycle model requires funding of ₹1,500 crore, it computes. Given current market conditions, debt is the most optimal source. However, the Chairperson's speech for the upcoming Annual General Meeting proudly declares that the company is debt-free. This needs to be updated. Action initiated: the communications head, responsible for the address, is notified immediately.

Corporate espionage is real—and new product development ranks high among vulnerable areas. Fret not: quantum communication keeps your strategy safe.

While Amit takes center stage, Siddhartha, attending in person, enjoys his daily cold brew. He accidentally knocks over the glass, causing a deep gash on his left hand. Dr. Sen, the company doctor based in Kolkata, examines the wound virtually and concludes it needs two stitches. Thanks to telepresence robotics, Dr. Sen patches him up—despite being 1,600 kilometers away.

And through all this, you could be watching the next season of *Blacklist*. If there's a sudden twist in the meeting—a twist so unpredictable that even Gen AI can't handle it—the system nudges you. But let's be honest: very few meetings are *that* dramatic.

Now gear up for an even more disruptive leap—swapping avatars for 'clones.' Gen AI won't just mirror your verbal responses; it'll replicate your facial expressions, gestures, and body language too. As they say, send your avatar to work!

THE ANSWER: 42

In Douglas Adams' brilliant *Hitchhiker's Guide to the Galaxy*,[28] a race of hyper-intelligent, pan-dimensional beings create a supercomputer to find the answer to the ultimate question of life, the universe, and everything. After seven and a half million years of analysis, the answer is—42. The implications of the avatar-in-office trend are, fortunately, far less enigmatic, albeit revolutionary.

Increased productivity

Your avatar attends routine meetings, freeing your real self to focus on strategic or cutting-edge work—tasks worthy of human intelligence. Imagine a near-limitless number of clones accompanying you and everyone else to work. Organizational productivity would soar.

Missing: the human touch

The downside? Limited bonding with colleagues. In-person discussions demand your full attention—mind and body.

---

28 'The Hitchhiker's Guide to the Galaxy', Douglas Adams, first published by Pan Books in 1979

With Gen AI-enabled avatars, minimal attention suffices. But relationships require effort. Nonchalance and half-hearted presence are the antithesis of connection.

The best, each time

Capabilities and expertise, even within the same domain, vary across employees. The social media maestro may be based in Singapore, the branding expert in Düsseldorf, and the creative genius in Helsinki. Combining such talent from across the globe is now possible each time—not just as an exception. Sure, a video call could facilitate the same, but often with sub-optimal outcomes.

Advanced interactive and communication technologies now allow effective collaboration across borders. Engineers from different locations can work together to resolve, say, the vexing issue of high fuel consumption in an under-development car model. Gen AI simulates scenarios and proposes potential solutions. Extended reality and hologram technologies generate three-dimensional, interactive engine models. At the end of such exercises, the human engineers may or may not add to their own knowledge—but Gen AI certainly does. In a sense, this raises the bar each time.

Safety first

Telepresence robots, combined with Gen AI, reduce security risks in hazardous or unstable environments, significantly raising safety benchmarks within organizations.

JUMP-STARTING YOUR COMPANY

The multitude of technologies presents a quagmire of options. Follow these simple guidelines to avoid being caught in quicksand.

1. Identify relevant technologies

Deep technologies that facilitate communication and interactivity are abundant. Nearly all of them yield exponentially powerful outcomes when paired with Gen AI. However, not all may be relevant to your business—map the ones that are.

Keep in mind geography-specific practicalities and applications. This includes factors such as bandwidth or speed (for example, do the broadband networks in the location support holograms?). Depending on your organization's structure, certain functions may be geographically concentrated. For instance, if the company's engineering design hub is primarily in Germany and India, prioritize deploying technologies like Extended Reality in those regions—assuming practical feasibility.

2. Forge technology partnerships

Expecting in-house expertise across a multitude of advanced, fast-evolving technologies is unrealistic. Partner with technology providers and independent experts to assess the potential of each technology and its applicability to your business. Given the lightning-fast pace of change, review relevance regularly—not once every three to four years. Engage in multiple collaborations for a well-rounded view of current and emerging possibilities.

3. Undertake pilots

'The best-laid plans of mice and men oft' go awry', as Robert Burns[29] famous line in 'To a Mouse'[30] goes. Detailed planning is essential, but actual execution tells the real story. Prepare for high-relevance pilots by forming specialized teams and, crucially, allocating adequate funds. Keep in mind that not all pilots will succeed—that's the inherent nature of innovation and experimentation.

4. Train employees

Employee resistance and lack of proficiency are primary reasons for failed technology implementation. Introduce employees to emerging technologies even while you're still evaluating their contextual utility. Early involvement boosts buy-in. As a bonus, some of the best use-case ideas may come from employees themselves. While interfaces for most advanced technologies are intuitive—thanks in large part to Gen AI—a certain level of training is still necessary.

JUMP-STARTING YOUR CAREER

While organizations will drive the execution of this trend, here are two actions you can take to advance your own career.

---

29 Robert Burns, an 18th century poet and lyrist, is generally regarded as the national poet of Scotland. The quoted line was originally written in Scots language, the English translation of which has been provided above.

30 The poem appeared in 'Poems, Chiefly in the Scottish Dialect' (popularly referred to the Kilmarnock Edition), a collection of poems by Robert Burns, first printed and issued by John Wilson of Kilmarnock in July 1786

1. Up your tech-savviness quotient

Do your own homework. Familiarize yourself with the range of relevant technologies. Use your understanding of your organization to identify the most applicable ones—and prioritize learning and upskilling in those areas.

2. Be an early adopter

Building on the above, proactively identify use cases tailored to your role. This will help cement your position as a future-ready, tech-savvy team member.

CHAPTER 12

CONCLUSION

Gen AI is revolutionizing the way we conduct business, our professional dynamics, and who we need to be to thrive in the workplace. At a broader level, the zeitgeist is reshaping the very fabric of the corporate world, disrupting both the industry and organizational structure. The ten megatrends elaborated previously provide a preview into the transformations that lie ahead.

WHAT DOES IT ALL MEAN?

Brace for a paradigm shift as Gen AI redefines the business arena by propelling automation and decision-making. Introducing generative capabilities enables existing automation technologies to extend their purview to other functions. Further heightening and accelerating automation is Gen AI's superior analytical ability, stemming from its pattern recognition and creation functionalities. The result is a leap forward in data democratization: the democratization of logical decision-making. Gen AI can mimic human decision-making based on heuristics as well as our ability to choose an optimal option in situations of incomplete information, enabling systems to operate effectively under complex, real-life scenarios.

A similar approach allows Gen AI to determine the most effective modality for person-to-person interactions—calibrating tone and nuances to increase the likelihood of a desired outcome. In fact, combined with other deep technologies, Gen AI has the ability to generate a clone of you—not just in appearance, but also voice, turn of phrase, and, eerily, your typical reactions.

The implications for an organization are grave, concerning its strategy, structure, systems, and even its survival. In the new world, past glory is not an indicator of future success. Learning afresh and adaptability is the mantra for survival. Gen AI marks the demise of entire sectors, not just firms. Many traditional levers of competitive advantage become antiquated, giving rise to a new set of factors such as deep understanding of human psychology and behaviour, off-beat actions, trust, and experience, among others. This calls for an overhaul of corporate and functional strategy. Another strategic ramification of Gen AI's intuitiveness, ease-of-use, and tremendous capability is the potential to bring many outsourced activities back into the organization's fold. Tasks once contracted out due to lack of expertise or management bandwidth can now be accomplished with a click, opening up possibilities for in-sourcing.

Massive strategic rebuild implies radical changes in organizational structure. New roles necessitating non-conventional competences will emerge. Simultaneously, some positions may become redundant or merge with others (automation and advanced decision-making tools allow for a wider span of control). This could have a seismic impact on total employee strength and the shape of the hierarchy pyramid. Translating intent into effective action requires enabling systems and processes. Recruitment criteria, performance metrics, incentive structures, decision-making protocols, and risk management are just a few of the elements that need to be redesigned to ensure they are future-fit.

Rebuilding an organization has a domino effect on the individual—you. A fresh set of strategic drivers at the organizational level demands new competencies in employees: lateral thinking, high emotional and cultural quotient, and the ability to connect the dots are a few such skills. The unprecedented changes heralded by the imminent epoch offer an opportunity to reinvent yourself—to take on a vastly different role or pursue an unrelated field of expertise vis-à-vis your current specialism. Be prepared for a shift in your 'performance status': evolving expertise requirements could boost an average performer into the star category, and vice versa. Perhaps the most immediate impact on you personally is the need to either reskill or upskill—an imperative across all tiers of hierarchy, from board members and CEOs to recent entrants into the workforce.

IS THIS SCIENCE FICTION?

The tsunami is upon us. Gen AI is already embedded in the latest versions of mobile phones, internet search engines, and available as stand-alone apps for everyone to use. Unsurprisingly, the world of business is not far behind, with employees already leveraging the technology to generate drafts of proposals, image blueprints, and more. Although the current pace of full-fledged adoption across functions and activities may appear slow in some quarters, the momentum will amplify exponentially once the early movers are on board. Organizations—irrespective of sector or size—will be swept into this snowball effect. There is no immunity pill.

Human intervention is the only deterrent to Gen AI's swift progress and rapid mobilization. John Hopfield and Geoffrey Hinton, recently awarded the Nobel Prize in Physics for their pioneering work in machine learning, have issued warnings about the potential of AI, calling for strict vigilance against misuse and unintended consequences.[1] "I am worried that the overall consequence of this might be systems more intelligent than us that eventually take control," Hinton said. Hopfield signed a petition calling for strong control of the technology.

---

1 'Pioneers in artificial intelligence win the Nobel Prize in physics', AP News, 9 October 2024, Pioneers in artificial intelligence win the Nobel Prize in physics | AP News ; 'Nobel physics prize 2024 won by AI pioneers John Hopfield and Geoffrey Hinton', Reuters, 10 October 2024, Nobel physics prize 2024 won by AI pioneers John Hopfield and Geoffrey Hinton | Reuters ; 'Godfather of AI delivers a stark warning after winning Nobel in Physics', India Today, 8 October 2024, Godfather of AI delivers a stark warning after winning Nobel in Physics – India Today

Depending on the nature of oversight and controls instituted—if any—the pace of Gen AI adoption could dampen, triggering a domino effect on the realization of the mega-trends. At the same time, advancements in complementary deep technologies, as well as in Gen AI itself, could accelerate their materialization. Either way, leadership in every organization must conduct a hawk-eyed review of ethical, security, privacy, and related issues and safeguards.

WHAT NEXT?

As Artificial General Intelligence emerges, expect an entirely different set of mega-trends to appear.

New technologies complementary to Gen AI—whose combined effect redefines the prevailing reality—are another game-changer. One such technology is Brain-Computer Interface (also known as Brain-Machine Interface, BCI or BMI), a direct communication link between signals from the brain and an external device, such as a computer, robotic limb, or cursor.[2] BCI, in itself, is transformative, allowing people to 'directly' translate thought into actions like controlling a motorized wheelchair or writing a book without physically

---

2 'AI's Next Frontier: Are Brain-Computer Interfaces The Future Of Communication?', Forbes, 11 August 2023, AI's Next Frontier: Are Brain-Computer Interfaces The Future Of Communication? (forbes.com) ; 'brain-computer interface (BCI)', Tech Target, What is brain-computer interface (BCI)? | Definition from TechTarget ; 'Gen AI Impact Series-2- The Combined Power of Generative AI and Brain Computer Interface', Blog, 25 August 2023, (31) Gen AI Impact Series-2- The Combined Power of Generative AI and Brain Computer Interface (BCI) | LinkedIn

typing or using a mouse. Combined with Gen AI, the possibilities are mind-blowing: real-time problem-solving; instantaneous idea generation; personalized messaging based on real-time detection of a recipient's mood; brain-to-brain communication akin to telepathy; and thought-controlled virtual environments for gaming and learning, among others.

Needless to say, other technologies—equally disruptive or perhaps even more so—may emerge. Artificial Super Intelligence is one such example, with implications that are truly unsettling. Fortunately, current wisdom suggests that its emergence is still several decades away.

Meanwhile, companies and professionals would do well to reflect on the ten mega-trends presented here. Those who initiate action early are poised to win in the Gen AI era.

> *Generative AI's future is grand,*
> *Crafting wonders with just a command.*
> *But beware of the sway,*
> *It could lead us astray,*
> *If we don't keep control in our hand!*
>
> – Courtesy, ChatGPT[3]

---

3 ChatGPT, on being prompted to "create a limerick on the future of generative artificial intelligence, positive but also a word of caution. Created and retrieved on 10 October 2024

ACKNOWLEDGEMENTS

Heartfelt gratitude to Team Om Books International for your bravado in backing this book when it was still just a loosely structured prompt, fuelled by heroic large language model hallucinations.

And to Saba Umme Salma, my editor extraordinaire, for trimming and tightening my waffling prose. Your editorial wizardry wrestled coherence from text that read like it had been generated by an AI trained exclusively on emergency evacuation instructions penned by woke philosophers.

Mr Bhaskar Pramanik, I am overwhelmed by your foreword that makes me sound far wiser than I am (or possibly ever will be). Mr Manish Sabharwal, Prof. Pankaj Chandra and Prof. Rishikesha Krishnan: your words added gravitas and framed the content in a deeper, more meaningful way — I'm grateful and flattered, in equal measure, to each of you.

Lastly, to my dearest parents: thank you for everything — from the perfect blend of gentle encouragement to the not-so-gentle prodding to meet deadlines; for allowing me shirk chores and, crucially, not replacing me with a Gen AI-powered hologram. For your unwavering love – this one's for you.